·THE·
UNOFFICIAL
GAME OF
THRONES
COOKBOOK

·THE·
UNOFFICIAL
GAME OF
THRONES
COOKBOOK

From Direwolf Ale to Auroch Stew—
More Than 150 Recipes from
Westeros and Beyond

Alan Kistler, creator and co-host of *Crazy Sexy Geeks*

Adamsmedia
AVON, MASSACHUSETTS

Copyright © 2012 by F+W Media, Inc.
All rights reserved.
This book, or parts thereof, may not be reproduced in any
form without permission from the publisher; exceptions are
made for brief excerpts used in published reviews.

Published by
Adams Media, a division of F+W Media, Inc.
57 Littlefield Street, Avon, MA 02322. U.S.A.
www.adamsmedia.com

ISBN 10: 1-4405-3872-7
ISBN 13: 978-1-4405-3872-8
eISBN 10: 1-4405-3895-6
eISBN 13: 978-1-4405-3895-7

Printed in the United States of America.

10   9   8   7   6   5   4   3   2

Library of Congress Cataloging-in-Publication Data
is available from the publisher.

Always follow safety and commonsense cooking protocol while using kitchen utensils, operating ovens and stoves, and handling uncooked food. If children are assisting in the preparation of any recipe, they should always be supervised by an adult.

Interior illustrations © 123rf.com and istockphoto.com

This book is available at quantity discounts for bulk purchases.
For information, please call 1-800-289-0963.

Dedication

For my parents, Kevin and Lourdes.

Acknowledgments

First, I would like to thank my parents and brother Kevin, Jr., for helping during tough times, and my grandparents Alan and Marie Kistler for pushing me so much when I was younger. Second, Lisa McMullan must be thanked for her constant support and for putting up with my no doubt tiresome need for quiet and solitude during the process of researching and writing this book—when I know she would have preferred that I spend more time having fun with her instead.

Amy Ratcliffe, the biggest fan of A Song of Ice and Fire I know, proved invaluable in pointing me in the right directions here and there when I first began this book and was the first to speak to me about the series with such passion that I decided to finally see what all the fuss was about.

Kat Slayton and Jennifer Ewing were both very helpful friends, making sure to remind me to "get back to work" at odd hours of the day and night. I would be hard-pressed to find greater taskmasters who are able to scold so sweetly.

Brandi Bowles's efficiency and resourcefulness as an agent cannot be exaggerated and I am very lucky that she wound up coming into my life soon before this project took shape.

The contributions of Victoria Sandbrook are too numerous to explain and it is not hyperbole to say that without her trust in me and her thorough work, this volume would not exist at all.

Thanks to Adri Cowan, who took a chance and was kind enough to mention my name when she realized this was a project in need of an author.

And finally, thanks to George R. R. Martin for being one of those writers who builds a world so completely that even details such as the dishes served become essential parts of the story rather than mere background.

Contents

CHAPTER 3

SOMETHING OFF THE SIDEBOARD: SIDES AND BREAD ... 61

CHAPTER 4

FIRESIDE FARE: SOUPS, STEWS, AND SALADS ... 89

CHAPTER 5
FEASTS FOR FRIENDS—AND ENEMIES: MAIN COURSES . . . 133

CHAPTER 6
DECEITFUL DELIGHTS: DESSERTS, DRINKS, AND "POISONOUS" COCKTAILS . . . 189

APPENDIX A:
STANDARD BREWING PROCESSES . . . 235

APPENDIX B:
RECIPES BY REGION . . . 239

INDEX . . . 244

Introduction

"Winter is coming . . . "

That's enough to give you goosebumps, isn't it? The House of Stark's words put a chill in the air, a sensation of icy wind and perhaps even snow, of chapped lips and cold hands seeking warmth. Even if Winterfell is just in our imagination, it can still *feel* real.

George R. R. Martin has filled his series A Song of Ice and Fire with simple phrases and vivid passages that flood our minds with a torrent of feelings. Whether we're reading the books or watching the show, we're *in* Westeros in our minds. We envision ourselves sitting in the castles and fortresses of the Lannisters or the Starks. We ride with the Dothraki across a dreamscape. We feel the winds that blow at the top of the Wall, the bitter cold and the thinner atmosphere that somehow makes us more alert that out there, north of what we've come to know of the world, are creatures that should not exist and, worse, have taken notice of us.

Humans, no matter what nation they are from or what kind of family raised them, are innately sensual. We always find ways to carry ourselves to places and times beyond our physical reach. Indeed, food can whisk us away in one sip, one bite, one breath. The moment we open a bottle of well-aged wine, we are breathing in the air of those long-ago times, air that was inadvertently trapped by whoever bottled the wine in the first place. When we eat a meal "from the old country," we can imagine— in some corner of our mind where imagination keeps its best knick-knacks and mementos—that we are transported back, whether we've been there or not. We can imagine some aspect of how our ancestors lived because we know their food. We hunger for the fanciful and sate it with a bite of reality—so why not do the same for the fantasy of Westeros?

With a book or show to guide you, you can picture the keep of Winterfell and see how it relates to the lands around it, but why not experience its flavors and smells, too? Let lobster and snails seat you in the Stark's dining hall. Let the scent and taste of fire-roasted meat draw up a chair next to Drogo's tent so you can listen as he recounts conquests of old and conquests yet to come. Pour spiced wine or a darker beverage and grin mischievously as you imagine yourself a warrior or an assassin.

In Martin's world, however, food means more; it is connected to the characters themselves and can be a respite from reality, a means of survival, or simply another pawn in the greater game. For Arya, a lemon cake is not just a dessert. As tragedy strikes, the treat becomes a symbol of a happier, seemingly simpler time, a taste of summer despite looming winter. For many characters, meals are the only times when they are able to have some peace and quiet amid political and personal chaos. Some of them know that each meal may not just be important . . . it could also be their last.

Each recipe includes a description of the scene; a discussion of characters, themes, or settings related to the food; and the book and chapter in which the food appears. In some cases, the recipes have been inspired by the characters and scenes, as well as other food and beverages. Brynden Tully's Blackened Trout with Dornish Gremolata (Chapter 5) and Direwolf Ale (Chapter 6), for example, may not have been mentioned in the books, but they still bring out the flavor of the fictional world. We hope readers will forgive artistic license taken and accept them in the spirit they are intended.

(And don't worry: spoilers have been avoided!)

Enjoy!

CHAPTER 1

HEROIC MORNINGS:
Breakfasts for Warriors

The world that encompasses and surrounds Westeros is very different from our own. True, many of its people and customs seem familiar, as if borrowed from our history and the legends of our past. But it is clearly another world with its own stories and legacies, where dragons are not simply the product of imagination and where dead men may do more than tell tales.

But while the Seven Kingdoms and the lands beyond the Wall may hold strange and magical creatures, the men and women who inhabit this world are just that: men and women like us. They bleed, they sleep, and they hunger. After hours of sleep, their bodies need nourishment, especially if it could be an entire day before they have another meal. Bran Stark and his father Eddard may eat a pleasing breakfast to ease their minds after troubling dreams. Jon Snow eats to gain enough strength so that he'll not tire during his training and duties in the harsh Northern climate. Tyrion Lannister breaks his fast with savory tastes as a means of relaxing before he's forced to face whatever cruel new obstacles await. Arya sees breakfast as a necessary chore to deal with before the exciting work can begin. The Dothraki take breakfast as they enjoy all pleasures: passionately.

Across cultures and even across worlds, we all can relate to the emotions and sensations of beginning the day with a fine meal, either as a moment of peace before the day begins or as a deliberate intake of energy that we know we'll need later. The morning dishes offered here are sure to satisfy whatever needs you have when you rise in the morning.

LAST BITE OF SUMMER BLACKBERRY PRESERVES

In times past, this treat was seen as a healing agent that could help with weakness and disease. Winterfell's cook Gage would likely keep plenty of sweet options on hand to chase away anxiety and illness. This preserve will brighten a morning—or ward off worry about things that go bump in the night. (*A Game of Thrones*, Chapter 14—Catelyn)

MAKES ABOUT 6 PINTS

3 quarts blackberries
7½ cups granulated sugar
2 (3-ounce) pouches liquid
   pectin

1. Rinse fully ripe blackberries in cold water and drain.
2. Place blackberries into a stockpot.
3. Crush with a potato masher to extract juice. Stir in the sugar and mix well.
4. Bring to a full rolling boil over high heat, stirring constantly.
5. Add pectin and return to a full rolling boil. Boil hard for 1 minute. Remove from heat.
6. Skim off foam. Ladle preserves into sterilized Mason jars. Wipe rims. Cap and seal. Place on a rack in a water-bath canner or a large stockpot with a lid. Cover jars 1–2 inches with boiling water. Put a lid on the bath or pot and begin timing when water is boiling; boil for 5 minutes. Remove jars with a jar lifter and place them on a towel-covered counter to cool. Leave undisturbed for 12–24 hours. Check the seals and remove the screwbands.
7. Serve preserves on toast with butter and honey.

A WORD OF WISDOM

Canning your own food can produce delicious results, but always make sure you're familiar with the best practices and tools necessary for safe and successful canning before you jump in. Put food safety first: your work area should be clean and you should never skimp on processing times or you could risk contaminating your food. Mason jars with tight-fitting lids are the only ones suitable to use when canning as they are intended for multiple uses (unlike commercial food jars) and are made with materials considered food-safe by modern standards (unlike antique canning jars).

Northmen's Soft-Boiled Eggs and Bacon

In the colder climates of the North, the vegetable harvest becomes more scarce and more important as the next winter approaches. Fortunately, pigs and chickens can be kept year-round to provide food. Noble lords and ladies of Westeros and stable boys alike would enjoy this commonplace breakfast alongside fire-toasted Winterfell Black Bread (Chapter 3), a dollop of jam, and a mug of cider. (*A Game of Thrones*, Chapter 14—Catelyn)

SERVES 2

6 slices of bacon
2 pasteurized eggs, any size

1. Place bacon in a pan, laying pieces side by side without overlapping.
2. Cook bacon on medium heat for approximately 10 minutes or until edges brown and curl.
3. Flip bacon once and continue to cook until it reaches your desired level of crispiness. Remove bacon from pan and set aside on a plate covered with a paper towel.
4. Fill a pot with enough cold water so that there will be at least ½ inch of water above the eggs. Bring the water to a rolling boil. Place the eggs in the pot and cook for 3 to 5 minutes (depending on your own preference for soft-boiled eggs).
5. Remove the eggs from the pot and place in cold water until cool enough to handle.
6. Serve bacon and peeled eggs together with toasted bread.

A Word of Wisdom

Timing boiled eggs is a matter of much debate. Many suggest 3–6 minutes for a soft yolk, 6–8 minutes for a medium yolk, and 8–10 minutes for a firm yolk. You may want to invest in an egg pricker, which will allow a little air to escape the egg as it boils, preventing it from cracking.

Black Brothers' Blood Sausage Breakfast

Life in the Night's Watch isn't easy. Long hours of patrol and training mean the hours between food and sleep can grow longer and longer. Blood sausage breakfast would help Brothers of the Watch keep energy up on even the coldest days, and the ingredients keep well in cold storage through the long nights. (*A Game of Thrones*, Chapter 48—Jon)

SERVES 4

4 blood sausages, sliced
   into medallions
2 tablespoons butter
4 yellow onions, sliced into
   half-rings
4 apples, cored and sliced
   (preferably Jonathan,
   Jonagold, or Golden
   Delicious)

1. Cook sausages in 1 tablespoon of the butter in a frying pan on medium-high for about 20 minutes, turning every 5 minutes, until casing is crispy and browned. Remove sausages from pan and set aside.
2. Add remaining butter to pan and fry onions and apples together on medium-high until apples are golden brown.
3. Serve sausages, onions, and apples together.

A Word of Wisdom

Blood sausage also goes very nicely with sides such as mashed potatoes, lingonberry jam, crusty bread, or a plate of steamed vegetables.

TYWIN LANNISTER'S GARLIC SAUSAGE

More summery than its black Northern cousin, garlic sausage would be much more common among Lord Tywin Lannister's troops. A knight's life of constant travel and isolation requires food that stores well and can be prepared quickly, in case a speedy departure is needed. Whether requiring a main dish for a journey through the countryside or enjoying the comfort of home, this is a recipe you'll want to know. (*A Game of Thrones*, Chapter 62—Tyrion)

SERVES 10

2½ pounds chicken
¼–½ pound pork fat
½ bulb garlic
1 yellow onion
½ bunch fresh oregano, chopped
Freshly cracked black pepper to taste
Kosher salt to taste
1 tablespoon butter or cooking oil

1. Grind the meat and fat separately. Keep chilled. Peel and mince the garlic and onion.
2. Mix together all the ingredients except butter in a chilled bowl with chilled utensils. If using an electric mixer, be sure not to overblend the meat and fat.
3. Either stuff the mixture into casings or form into patties.
4. Heat butter or oil to medium temperature in a large sauté pan. Add the sausage, cover, and cook for about 30 minutes, turning at 5-minute intervals. Uncover and cook for 10 to 15 minutes, until thoroughly browned.

A WORD OF WISDOM

There's more to homemade sausage than the option to choose the meats and flavors you get to feature. Grind the meat and fat in your own kitchen or buy ground goods from a butcher. Pick your preferred casing or make patties in a pinch. Just keep the meat and fat ice-cold throughout the process to ensure food safety.

Sansa's Buttermilk Biscuits

Lady Sansa Stark sipped buttermilk *with* her biscuits, but the two can be combined into a classic breakfast treat. Fluffy and rich, these biscuits are reminiscent of the life Sansa thought she had and the dream she believed was destined to become her future reality. Served warm and fresh with a fried breakfast, these just might remind anyone of safer, happier times. (*A Game of Thrones*, Chapter 67—Sansa)

MAKES 12–15 BISCUITS

2 cups all-purpose flour
4 teaspoons baking powder
¼ teaspoon baking soda
¾ teaspoon plus 1 pinch kosher salt
¼ cup (½ stick) cold unsalted butter
1 cup cold buttermilk
1 egg
1 tablespoon water

1. Line a baking sheet with parchment or lightly grease the sheet. In a large bowl, sift together flour, baking powder, baking soda, and ¾ teaspoon salt. Cut in butter until it is broken down into pea-size pieces.
2. Make a well in the center of the flour mixture, and pour in buttermilk. Using a fork, blend the flour mixture and buttermilk until the dough just comes together.
3. Turn onto a floured surface and fold dough over onto itself 6–8 times. (Be careful not to knead or overwork.) Pat into 1-inch thickness. Cut into circles using a floured round cutter. Place biscuits 2 inches apart on prepared pan and set aside to rest 10–15 minutes. Preheat oven to 425°F.
4. Mix egg with a pinch of salt and 1 tablespoon water. Brush lightly onto biscuits, then bake 15–20 minutes, until golden brown. Turn pan halfway through baking to promote even browning.

A Word of Wisdom

Make sure the buttermilk you use for these biscuits is fresh. Buttermilk can spoil quickly and you don't want to ruin the flavor of your treats! If you don't think you'll use enough buttermilk to warrant buying a whole container, buy powdered buttermilk instead. It stays fresh much longer.

Dothraki Antelope and Spicy Sausage

The meat used in sausage changes between the diverse regions of Westeros and Essos, making it a food fit for many tastes. Lamb, antelope, and horse meat are just a few varieties that grace tables noble and rustic. Daenerys Targaryen may turn such food away because her mind is troubled by where her new marriage might take her life, but other characters enjoy the spiced meat for breakfast, lunch, or dinner, and you should as well. This particular sausage with antelope caught in the Dothraki Sea makes a fine brunch dish and can bring out the Dothraki within. (*A Game of Thrones*, Chapter 11—Daenerys)

SERVES 8–10

½ pound ground antelope
  or venison
½ pound spicy breakfast
  sausage
Kosher salt and freshly
  ground pepper
2 (4-ounce) cans green
  chilies, chopped
1 cup shredded Monterey
  jack cheese
12 eggs
1½ cups whole milk
Salsa, sour cream,
  chopped green onions
  (for serving)

1. Preheat oven to 350°F. Grease large baking dish and set aside.
2. Brown meat and place evenly in the baking dish. Season to taste with salt and pepper. Sprinkle green chilies, then cheese, evenly over meat.
3. With the back of a spoon, slightly hollow 12 places for the eggs (away from the edge of the baking dish). Break eggs into the indentations and lightly break yolks with a fork. Pour milk over all and bake for about 30 to 40 minutes, just until set.
4. Serve with salsa, sour cream, and chopped green onions on the side.

A Word of Wisdom

Of course, game breakfast sausage works just as well and, like any good meal, is fit for a feast among peasants or nobility. If you need more spice (and what warrior doesn't?), throw on some fennel, red pepper flakes, a few drops of hot sauce, or additional chilies.

NORTHERN HARVEST OAT BISCUITS

As Bran and his guests would attest, oat biscuits serve as welcome additions to any breakfast or harvest feast, acting as commonplace snacks yet subtly complementing the flavor of other dishes. Serve these flavorful scones on their own with a piping hot mug of breakfast tea. Or enjoy them later in the day with Harrenhal Vegetable Stew (Chapter 4), Littlefinger's Lamprey Pie (Chapter 5), Brynden Tully's Blackened Trout with Dornish Gremolata (Chapter 5), or a Stag Strongwine Snifter (Chapter 6). (*A Clash of Kings*, Chapter 16—Bran)

MAKES 6–8 SCONES

1 cup Scottish oats

1½ cups milk

1 egg

1 teaspoon vanilla extract

1 cup cake flour

½ cup oat flour

½ teaspoon ground cinnamon

½ teaspoon kosher salt

2 teaspoons baking powder

1½ cups brown sugar

½ cup (1 stick) unsalted butter, diced and well chilled

1 egg yolk

½ cup cream

Northern Harvest Oat Biscuits

(CONTINUED)

1. Combine oats and 1 cup milk. Refrigerate overnight to soften.
2. Preheat oven to 375°F. Line a baking sheet with parchment or lightly grease the sheet. In a small bowl, whisk together the egg, vanilla, and remaining ½ cup milk; set aside. In a large bowl, sift together cake flour, oat flour, cinnamon, salt, baking powder, and ½ cup brown sugar.
3. Cut the chilled butter into the dry ingredients, breaking it into small, pea-size pieces with your fingertips or a pastry blender. Be sure not to mix too much. Butter and flour should create a dry, crumbly mixture, not a paste.
4. Make a well in the center of the flour-butter mixture. Add the egg mixture and the soaked oats. Stir gently until just moistened. Turn the dough onto a lightly floured work surface and fold it 7 or 8 times, until it holds together. (Do not knead.) Flatten the dough into a disk 1-inch thick. Cut the disk into 6–8 wedges and place them on the prepared pan, evenly spaced.
5. Whisk together the yolk and cream and brush it generously on the top of each scone. Sprinkle the tops with remaining brown sugar. Allow scones to rest 10 minutes and then bake until golden brown, about 15 minutes.

A Word of Wisdom

The wedge shape used in this recipe recalls a time when baking focused on sustenance rather than any concern with appearance. Today's scones are often cut out of the dough like biscuits or formed into decorative shapes. This practice is fine but also results in some wasted dough, something that bakers of past centuries (and likely in Westeros) would not have tolerated.

DIREWOLF BEEF AND BACON PIE

The sigil of the House of Stark is the direwolf, a beast that is much larger and more fearsome than any other canine predator found in nature. With such a noble carnivore on their shields, it is no wonder that the Starks seem to enjoy meats at every meal, even at the start of the day. Direwolf Beef and Bacon Pie makes for a hearty, savory breakfast for anyone, wolf or not. (*A Game of Thrones*, Chapter 70—Jon)

SERVES 4

12 slices bacon
1 pound ground beef
1 small onion, diced
2 carrots, peeled and diced
1 celery stalk, sliced
2 tablespoons vegetable oil
½ cup chopped
   mushrooms
2 tablespoons flour
1¼ cups beef broth
1 tablespoon
   Worcestershire sauce
¼ cup heavy cream
½ cup peas, fresh or frozen
Salt and pepper to taste
2 cups shredded potatoes
¼ cup mayonnaise
1 cup shredded Cheddar
   cheese
Pinch paprika

1. Preheat oven to 375°F.
2. Cook bacon, remove from pan, and set aside. Chop into small pieces. Brown the ground beef, remove from pan, and set aside.
3. Sauté the onion, carrots, and celery in the vegetable oil for 5 minutes over medium heat. Add the mushrooms and cook 5 more minutes, then add the meat back to the pan. Break up any large chunks of meat.
4. Sprinkle the meat mixture with the flour, stir, then add the beef broth and Worcestershire sauce. Simmer until thickened, stir in the cream and peas, and season with salt and pepper. (Use extra pepper and add some hot sauce if you want to spice up the pie.) Pour the mixture into a casserole dish.
5. Mix the shredded potatoes, mayonnaise, and cheese together in a bowl and then spread over the mixture in the dish.
6. Sprinkle the potatoes with paprika and bake for 30 minutes.

A WORD OF WISDOM

Refrigerate any meat pie or quiche soon after baking to ensure they are safe to eat. Cool the pie on the counter until just warm, cover it with plastic or foil, then place it in the refrigerator. If kept well chilled, it should last for two days.

WEASEL'S OATCAKES

The girl known as Weasel at Harrenhal has always been strong and smart for her age, but the ease with which she accepts a simple existence may be the thing that keeps her out of harm's way. Oatcakes fuel her long days of hard, physical work, and the little dash of dried apricots in this recipe would be a true treat on a dull morning, especially for someone just trying to blend in. (*A Clash of Kings*, Chapter 38—Arya)

SERVES 8

3 cups rolled oats

2 cups flour

¼ teaspoon baking soda or
  powder

1 egg white

⅓ cup plain yogurt

½ cup sugar

½ cup honey

½ teaspoon vanilla extract

½ cup dried apricots,
  chopped

1. Preheat oven to 325°F. Line a baking sheet with parchment or lightly grease the sheet.
2. Pulse the oats in a food processor 10 times, then add the flour and baking soda or powder and pulse to mix.
3. In a bowl, whisk the egg white until frothy, then add the yogurt, sugar, honey, and vanilla. Add the oat mixture and dried apricots to the yogurt mixture. Mix with a wooden spoon.
4. Roll the mixture into 8 balls and flatten them into thick, cylindrical patties.
5. Place the oatcakes on prepared baking sheet and bake for 15–20 minutes. Let cool and then refrigerate unless eating right away.

A Word of Wisdom

For a crunchier treat, replace the apricot with ½ cup chopped nuts. Or, just trade ¼ cup of apricots for ¼ cup of nuts to enjoy both. You can serve your oatcakes cold and any time of the day, but they're lovely hot with a pat of butter and syrup.

DRAGONSTONE MEAT AND MASH

Sitting in the dark dungeons below the castle of Dragonstone, Ser Davos Seaworth ponders life and death with relief only coming through regular meals. Meat and mash is one of the dishes that keeps him healthy. This warm, home-style meal of rich sausage, potatoes, and gravy belies his captivity. (*A Storm of Swords*, Chapter 25—Davos)

SERVES 4

4 large potatoes

Water to cover potatoes, plus 1 cup water

Pinch salt

1 tablespoon oil

8 Cumberland sausage links

2 tablespoons flour

1 cup milk

4 tablespoons (½ stick) butter or margarine

About 2½ tablespoons cream

Salt and pepper to taste

1 teaspoon dried or 2 teaspoons chopped fresh parsley, optional

Dragonstone Meat and Mash

(CONTINUED)

1. Wash and peel the potatoes, then cut into quarters.
2. Fill a medium-size saucepan with enough salted water to cover the potatoes, and bring to a boil over medium-high heat. Cook the potatoes in the boiling water until tender and easily pierced with a fork, about 20 minutes.
3. While potatoes are cooking, heat oil in a frying pan on medium-high. Prick sausage casings to prevent them from splitting, and cook sausages until brown. Remove sausages from pan and set aside.
4. Lower heat to medium and add 2 tablespoons of flour to pan drippings. Whisk carefully until flour is browned. Slowly whisk in milk and then 1 cup water until drippings from pan are well combined with liquid. Cook until gravy thickens.
5. When potatoes are soft and easily pierced with a fork, drain the saucepan.

6. Place the potatoes in a bowl and add the butter or margarine. Use a fork or potato masher to whip the potatoes until fluffy. Add the cream as you mix, being sure not to add more than is needed. Stir in salt and pepper to taste.
7. Serve sausages on top of potatoes. Drizzle with gravy, and dress with parsley if desired.

A Word of Wisdom

Though less traditional for the region, you can substitute just about any meat-and-gravy combination for a good, hearty breakfast. Leftovers from a feast of auroch steak or roast boar might give you everything you need for this sturdy plate of proteins and starch to break your fast.

Septa Mordane's Porridge

Even in the plush Red Keep, the good and kind Septa Mordane enjoys a simple breakfast rather than something extravagant or worldly. This porridge—gussied up with dried fruit, spice, and honey—would meet her approval *and* bring a smile to her usually serious countenance. And she certainly wouldn't fault you for adding a little creamy almond milk!

(*A Game of Thrones*, Chapter 44—Sansa)

SERVES 4

2 cups water
1 cup rolled oats
¼ teaspoon salt
½ cup dried currants
1 teaspoon ground
  cinnamon
4 teaspoons honey
2 tablespoons cream
1 cup almond milk, chilled

1. Bring water to a boil. Add the oats and salt and stir. Turn the heat to low and simmer 5 minutes.
2. Stir in the currants and simmer for 10 minutes, stirring occasionally.
3. Remove from heat and spoon cooked oatmeal into four bowls.
4. Sprinkle ¼ teaspoon cinnamon and drizzle 1 teaspoon honey on oatmeal in each bowl.
5. Mix the cream with the cold almond milk and serve it on the side in a small pitcher.

A Word of Wisdom

Oats have been enjoyed throughout civilized history, and remain an important part of a healthy diet. Threshing oats removes the hard, outer chaff, and winnowing separates out the edible oat from the chaff. Because oats lose only the outer husk during the milling process, they are more nutritious than refined wheat.

BACK AT THE WALL THICK CREAM OF WHEAT

Samwell may have been considered an embarrassment to the Tarly name, but his life in the Night's Watch is a chance for purpose. When he finds himself unprepared to travel the dark paths ahead, Three-Finger Hobb's unforgettable breakfast is like an island in his storm. One bite of this hot cereal is fortification against daily foes—and is a meal that makes it worth fighting to reach home again. (*A Storm of Swords*, Chapter 33—Samwell)

SERVES 1

⅔ cup milk
1 cup Cream of Wheat
  or farina
Honey to taste
Butter to taste

1. Heat milk on medium in a heavy saucepan until bubbles form on edges. Do not boil the milk.
2. Stir in Cream of Wheat. Cook on low, stirring occasionally, for 15–20 minutes, until wheat is thick and milk is well combined.
3. Serve in a bowl with honey and butter to taste.

A WORD OF WISDOM

Farina is simply a coarsely ground wheat cereal. Though it's best known as a breakfast cereal, you can also cook it like polenta as a side dish for other meals.

Night's Watch Breakfast Loaf

On the Wall, the Black Brothers can always rely on Three-Finger Hobb to keep their strength replenished. Practical and flavorful, this loaf packs sweet fruit and hearty nuts together to stave off the Brothers' hunger as long as possible. (*A Storm of Swords*, Chapter 55—Jon)

MAKES 1 LARGE LOAF (15–20 SLICES)

1½ cups plus 1 tablespoon water

½ cup honey

1¾ teaspoons active dry yeast (1 package)

3 eggs

¼ cup canola oil

1 teaspoon kosher salt

4–5 cups bread flour

1 tablespoon ground cinnamon

1 teaspoon ground nutmeg

1 teaspoon ground ginger

¼ teaspoon ground cloves

¾ cup dried apples, chopped

¾ cup golden raisins

½ cup pine nuts

NIGHT'S WATCH BREAKFAST LOAF

(CONTINUED)

1. In a large bowl, combine 1½ cups water, 2 tablespoons honey, and yeast. Stir to dissolve and let stand until foamy, about 10 minutes.

2. Add 2 eggs, oil, salt, and enough bread flour to create a firm dough. Turn onto a floured surface and knead 8–10 minutes. Add flour only to reduce stickiness. Return to bowl, dust the top lightly with flour, and cover with plastic wrap.

3. Rise at room temperature until doubled in volume, about 2–3 hours. Punch dough down, fold in half, and rise again, until doubled, about 45 minutes.

4. Coat a baking sheet with pan spray. Turn risen dough onto a floured surface and with a rolling pin, roll into an 18" × 24" rectangle. Warm remaining honey and brush over entire surface. Mix together cinnamon, nutmeg, ginger, and cloves, and sprinkle over honey. Evenly distribute apples, raisins, and pine nuts over the spices. Starting on a long edge, roll the dough up into a log. Join both ends of the log to make a circle, and place on baking sheet, seam-side down. Cover with plastic wrap, and rise again 30 minutes.

5. Preheat oven to 325°F. Combine remaining egg with the remaining tablespoon of water and brush over the surface of the bread. Slice two-thirds of the way into the log every 2 inches all round the ring. Turn each slice at a slight angle, so the resulting ring looks like a flower. Bake until golden brown and firm, about 50–60 minutes. Cool completely before slicing.

A WORD OF WISDOM

Too little yeast means that your bread won't rise properly. Too much, and it will simply collapse in the end. It's important to watch the dough as it rises and bakes. Don't be afraid to open the oven and check. If it isn't rising, your yeast may be past its expiration date or the room or oven may be too cold. Heating your oven slightly or placing the bowl on a heating pad set to low may help your dough rise.

FIERY DORNISH FRITTATA

In the Queen's Ballroom, the guests break their fast with this hot plate before a feast of seventy-seven courses. As Tyrion Lannister jokes, there's "nothing like a hearty breakfast to whet one's appetite" for food to follow. Under the shadow of the Queen, Sansa is fearful of the future and what plans are being made for her, and Tyrion's jokes hide deep concerns. When there's such an air of foreboding, a tasty dish can help alleviate one's spirits and calm the nerves for what tasks are yet to come. (*A Storm of Swords*, Chapter 59—Sansa)

SERVES 6–8

4 tablespoons olive oil, divided

6 large mushrooms, sliced (about 1¼ cups)

¼ cup chopped onion

1 red chili pepper, chopped

3 large eggs

½ cup milk

⅛ teaspoon nutmeg

Salt and freshly cracked pepper to taste

1 small tomato, chopped

¾ cup grated cheese, such as Cheddar

6–8 slices French bread, toasted

FIERY DORNISH FRITTATA

(CONTINUED)

1. Heat 2 tablespoons of the olive oil in a frying pan over medium-low heat. Add the mushrooms, onion, and red chili. Cook until the onion is tender. Remove from pan and set aside. Clean the pan.

2. Lightly beat the eggs with the milk. Stir in the nutmeg, salt, and pepper. Stir in the cooked mushrooms, onion, and chili pepper, the tomato, and ½ cup of the grated cheese.

3. Heat the remaining 2 tablespoons olive oil in the frying pan on medium-low heat. Swirl the oil around the pan to coat the pan entirely. Pour the egg mixture into the pan. Move the vegetables around if necessary to make sure they are evenly mixed throughout the egg.

4. Cook the frittata, uncovered, over medium-low heat. Tilt the pan occasionally or lift edges of the frittata with a spatula so that the uncooked egg runs underneath.

5. When the frittata is firm on top, cover the frying pan with a lid or plate. Turn the pan over so that the frittata falls onto the lid. Return the pan to the stovetop and slide the frittata back into the pan, so that the bottom of the frittata is on top. Sprinkle the remaining ¼ cup of grated cheese over the frittata. Cook over medium-low heat until the cheese is melted and the frittata is cooked through.

6. To serve, cut the frittata pizza-style into wedges and serve on top of the toasted French bread.

A WORD OF WISDOM

Don't worry if the frittata falls apart the first few times you try to make it. It can take a few tries to know when it's firm enough to turn over. Besides, a little breakage won't affect the taste!

HARD-AS-CERSEI BOILED EGGS, BREAD, AND HONEY

Queen Cersei is known for her cold rage and quick temper. When plans do not go as she intends, it is those around her who suffer, and only a fool would expect mercy or sympathy from the woman. Yet, when making sure to calm herself so she can find a new solution, Cersei Lannister knows a good way to start is with a fine breakfast. Who would dare argue with a Queen's logic? (*Feast of Crows*, Chapter 12—Cersei)

SERVES 1

2 eggs, any size
2 slices of bread, such as
   Westerosian Barley Bread
   or Inn at the Crossroads
   7-Grain Loaf (Chapter 3)
Honey to taste

1. Place the eggs in a saucepan and cover with cold water to at least ½ inch above the eggs. Cover the pot with the lid and bring to a rolling boil over high heat.
2. As soon as the water is boiling, remove from heat. Let the eggs stand in the hot water for 17 to 20 minutes. Remove the eggs from the saucepan and place in a bowl filled with cold water for at least 2 minutes, or until cool enough to handle. Peel off the shells.
3. Serve with slices of bread drizzled with honey to taste.

A WORD OF WISDOM

The trick to perfect hard-boiled eggs is to start with cold water. As soon as the water has boiled, remove the eggs from the burner.

WESTEROSIAN FRIED BREAKFAST

Many folks across Westeros agree: fried foods are delicious! Characters throught the land enjoy plates of fried eggs and meat when they wake up. This Westerosian breakfast has fed Ned Stark at King Robert's table, Jon Snow at the Wall, Jaime Lannister at the Inn of the Kneeling Man, and many other adventurers and warriors of the Seven Kingdoms.

SERVES 2

6 slices bacon

4 sausage links

4 duck eggs

2 slices of bread, lightly
  buttered on both sides

Freshly ground salt and
  pepper to taste

1. Place bacon in a pan, laying pieces side by side without overlapping.
2. Cook bacon on medium heat for approximately 10 minutes or until edges brown and curl.
3. Flip bacon once and continue to cook until it reaches your desired level of crispiness. Remove bacon from pan and set aside on a plate covered with a paper towel. Leave drippings in pan.
4. Prick sausage casings and cook on medium heat in the same pan until casings are well browned. Remove sausages from pan and set aside with bacon. Leave drippings in pan.
5. Crack eggs into the same pan. Cook on medium until bottoms set. Flip eggs over and continue to cook until edges pull away from pan and yolk is at desired firmness. Use a spatula to remove eggs from pan and set them aside. Leave drippings in pan.
6. Lay slices of bread in the same pan and lightly fry in drippings until both sides are golden.
7. Serve together with freshly ground salt and pepper to taste.

A WORD OF WISDOM

If you are watching your fat intake, lean smoked ham or prosciutto can be substituted for bacon.

THE BLIND GIRL'S PIPING HOT FISH AND PEPPER BREAKFAST

In the House of Black and White, there is no common language and many perform their work and pursue their agendas without sharing anything—except Umma's food. The child known as the Blind Girl may not understand much more than the cook's name and delicious cooking, but this dish of fish and pepper says it all.
(*A Dance with Dragons*, Chapter 45—The Blind Girl)

SERVES 4

¾ cup mayonnaise

Zest and juice of 1 lemon

1 clove garlic, minced

1 cup cornmeal

½ cup flour

1 teaspoon salt

1 teaspoon pepper

½ cup vegetable oil or more

2 large green tomatoes

2 pounds catfish fillets, skinless

2 jalapeño peppers, sliced

1. Combine mayonnaise, lemon, and garlic in a bowl and whisk to blend. Set aside.
2. Combine cornmeal, flour, salt, and pepper in a bowl large enough for dredging.
3. Heat vegetable oil in a large skillet over medium-high heat.
4. Slice green tomatoes ½-inch thick and dredge in cornmeal mixture. Place in the skillet and cook until brown on each side, about 3 or 4 minutes per side. Remove and keep warm.
5. Dredge fillets in the cornmeal mixture. Place in skillet with jalapeño peppers and fry until fish is golden brown, about 3 or 4 minutes per side, depending on how thick the fillets are. Add more oil as needed. Serve catfish and tomatoes with the mayonnaise sauce on the side.

A Word of Wisdom

Never refreeze fish or seafood. If you must store it in the refrigerator, tightly wrap or place in an airtight container for no more than 2 days.

CHAPTER 2

A MORSEL IN A MOMENT:
Appetizers and Snacks

T ravel is never easy in Westeros and Essos. The Kingsroad, the High Road, the Ocean Road, the River Road—even the Valyrian demon road—all wind through wild forests, barren wastes, and enemy territory. Those with political value must travel incognito at certain times, trusting no one, staying in no place for too long, and straying far from expected paths. Arya, Catelyn, Tyrion, Ser Barristan the Bold, and Quentyn Martell are just a few of those who must hide their identity on their journeys. The rangers of the Night's Watch rely on stealth to escape the notice of those who live in the wild, uncharted lands beyond the Wall. On the move, they must be ready to face Wildlings more accustomed to the ways of the forest than the civilized ways of the kneelers, and to evade greater foes who can move unseen and unheard through the land. Though travelers may enjoy roast swan at a wedding feast, they're not likely to carry leftovers on their backs for long miles.

The serving of appetizers is a mark of civilized, privileged culture. Dinner guests don't need to wait for the true meal to begin to start enjoying their host's hospitality, but simple folk may not have the means or need to worry about food *before* a precious meal. These small plates put people at ease and relax their defenses enough to inspire trust and unguarded discussion. It can be difficult to spark honest conversation at tense meetings, and the simple, shared enjoyment of a tasty morsel can be just enough to begin a dialogue.

The portions might be small, but this food can start new friendships, seal peace treaties, and keep an enemy (or death) at bay for one more day. Never mistake these morsels for being unimportant.

GRAND MAESTER PYCELLE'S PRIZED POMEGRANATE GRAPEFRUIT BARS

Pomegranate reminds Grand Maester Pycelle of the long summer in his youth, a time when the days were enjoyed with relaxation and fresh fruits. But the red, fine-tasting fruit also has great medicinal value—protecting the stomach, heart, eyes, and more—as do summery Dornish grapefruits, which are filled with vitamins and phytonutrients. Paired in this recipe, these practical fruits would breathe a hint of summer into any maester's day. (*A Game of Thrones*, Chapter 25—Eddard)

SERVES 10

2½ cups all-purpose flour

1¼ cups (2½ sticks) unsalted butter, softened

¾ cup confectioners' sugar

1 ripe pomegranate

5 eggs

½ cup fresh grapefruit juice

2½ cups granulated sugar

1¼ teaspoons baking powder

1. Preheat oven to 350°F. Mix together the flour, butter, and confectioners' sugar. Press into a large oblong baking pan and bake for 20 minutes. Remove from oven and let cool slightly.

2. While the crust bakes, cut open the pomegranate, remove the seeds, and set them aside. Discard the skin and other material.

3. Beat the eggs in a bowl, and mix in the grapefruit juice, sugar, and baking powder. Fold in the pomegranate seeds. Pour the mixture over the crust. Bake for 20 to 25 minutes, until the top is set. Allow to cool before cutting into bars.

A WORD OF WISDOM

Pomegranates are a versatile fruit that can be used as a garnish on sweet dishes. You can sprinkle the seeds over desserts and salads. When cutting them open or removing the pulp-encased seeds, be sure to wear an apron or your clothing could easily be stained.

King's Landing Snails in Garlic

For Sansa Stark, a dish of snails only enhances the majesty and novelty of visiting King's Landing and seeing her visions of fairy tales come true. In any setting—whether a joust or a feast—this dish transports tables away from the commonplace and familiar, with the snails served in delicious mushroom cups. Though Joffrey was at Sansa's side to accustom her to eating snails from their shells, this version of her gastronomic escape doesn't require a doting prince to enjoy. (*A Game of Thrones*, Chapter 29—Sansa)

SERVES 9

1 (28-ounce or 36-count)
   can escargot, drained and
   removed from their shells
½ cup (1 stick) butter
2 cloves garlic, minced
36 mushrooms, stems
   removed
½ cup white wine
½ cup cream
2 tablespoons all-purpose
   flour
Ground black pepper to
   taste

1. Preheat oven to 350°F. Lightly grease an escargot dish or a glass baking pan. If using an escargot dish, you may need to use several to prepare all escargot at once, depending on the size of your dish.
2. Soak escargot in cold water for 5 minutes.
3. Drain escargot and dry well with a paper towel. In a large skillet, melt butter over medium-high heat. Add garlic and sauté lightly. Before garlic browns, add escargot and mushroom caps. Stir often for about 5 minutes.
4. Whisk together wine, cream, flour, and pepper until smooth. Pour into skillet and bring to a light boil. Continue cooking, stirring often, until sauce thickens. Remove skillet from heat.
5. Spoon mushroom caps into escargot dish or baking dish, cap side down. Place one escargot into each cap. Spoon sauce evenly over each pair.
6. Bake for 10–15 minutes.

A Word of Wisdom

Escargot is used to refer both to the species of edible land snails used in fine cooking and to the dish made from them. These gastropods are actually cultivated for market through the practice of heliculture, though foragers also find them in some gardens, vineyards, and forests.

Robert's Fried Golden Goose Eggs

Eggs are a common part of breakfast across Westeros, but hale and hearty warriors may not be satisfied with a simple chicken egg. A goose-egg appetizer graces King Robert's plate on a day when he knows dangers are rising against his kingdom, but he and Ned Stark let themselves get lost in food and friendship anyway. This recipe offers the added delectable distraction of deep-fried breading and hearty sausage. (*A Game of Thrones*, Chapter 30—Eddard)

SERVES 4

Vegetable oil for deep-
   frying
¼ cup seasoned flour
4 hard-boiled goose eggs,
   peeled
1 pound ground sausage
1 goose egg, beaten
1 cup white bread crumbs

1. Heat the oil in a deep fryer to 350°F.
2. Place flour in a bowl and lightly roll each hard-boiled egg in the flour.
3. Divide the meat into fourths and flatten out into patties. Place each hard-boiled egg on a patty and carefully mold the meat around the egg, making sure there are no cracks.
4. Place beaten egg in a shallow bowl and bread crumbs in another shallow bowl. Roll meat-covered egg in the beaten egg and then in the bread crumbs until well covered.
5. Lower eggs into the hot oil and cook for about 5 to 6 minutes, until golden. Remove and set on a paper towel to drain. Cut into halves or quarters and serve.

A Word of Wisdom

Goose eggs require more special handling than their chicken-bred cousins, but are well worth it. They are a tad stronger than chicken eggs, and the taste will alter somewhat based on what the goose has been eating. If you're buying eggs from domesticated geese, this should not be a problem.

RED KEEP BLOOD ORANGE SAMPLER

This blood oranges sampler is a satisfying snack for nobles in the capitol. King Robert enjoys them not only for their taste, but for the memories they bring: happier, simpler times before the weight of the crown began to press on him. Arya enjoys them simply as a sweet-tasting treat when she's taking a break from lessons—and uses them as a weapon when Sansa is particularly annoying. An imported delicacy from warmer climates, the oranges seem to be taken for granted by those who can still afford the luxury of food and fond memories. (*A Game of Thrones,* Chapter 30—Eddard)

SERVES 4

2 blood oranges

1 teaspoon rose water

¼ cup pomegranate seeds

2 clementines or mandarin
   oranges

1. Slice the tops and bottoms off the blood oranges and set them on one of the cut surfaces.
2. With a sharp knife, cut the peel and pith off the oranges in downward strips around each orange to reveal the flesh. Cut the oranges into thin slices across the width, making round wheel slices. Remove any seeds.
3. Arrange the orange slices on four plates and sprinkle the rose water over them. Sprinkle the pomegranate seeds over the slices.
4. Peel the clementines and separate them into individual sections. Scatter the sections onto the blood oranges, dividing them among the four plates.

A WORD OF WISDOM

Clementines are tiny, seedless, easy-to-peel oranges that are similar to tangerines. The climate in Dorne is perfect for growing these gems.

Desperate Travelers' Acorn Paste

Whether they're braving the Kingsroad during war, fighting beyond the Wall, or foraging in the last days before the long winter, acorn paste can satisfy travelers' hunger. Even children have no problem preparing this food in a moment of need. This spread goes nicely on biscuits and bread—a luxury in the wild. (*A Clash of Kings*, Chapter 19—Arya)

SERVES 6

2 cups unbroken live oak acorns, shells removed

4–5 tablespoons peanut oil or other vegetable oil, divided use

1. Preheat oven to 350°F.
2. Coat acorns with 1 tablespoon peanut oil and spread on a cookie sheet. Bake for 10–15 minutes. Cool acorns.
3. Process the acorns in a food processor on high speed until finely ground. Continue processing until acorns form a thick paste.
4. Slowly add remaining peanut oil until smooth and creamy, scraping down sides and adding a little more oil as needed. Serve on Winterfell Black Bread, Trident Flax and Fennel Hardbread (both Chapter 3), or a bread of your choice.

A Word of Wisdom

Though acorn paste may be unfamiliar to anyone who hasn't needed to forage, other nut butters are commonplace. As an alternative to store-bought peanut butter, make your own almond, walnut, or macadamia butter. To prepare, just heat nuts of your choice in the oven at 400°F for 6–8 minutes or toast them on the stovetop in a dry skillet. A quick run through a food processor with a little oil will finish up the spread.

WINTERFELL COLD FRUIT SOUP

A harvest feast in a nobleman's keep naturally involves both fruits and vegetables from his land *and* exotic ingredients bought at great cost from traders and merchants. In the halls of Winterfell, the kitchen staff bring out a dish representing the North's bounty and the Stark family's wealth. Whether served as an appetizer or dessert, this soup might make it hard for guests to see the reality of the Starks' increasing weakness through the pretense of money and territory. (*A Clash of Kings*, Chapter 16—Bran)

SERVES 4

1 large mango, peeled and
   diced
2 cups fresh blueberries
1 cup sliced bananas
2 cups fresh strawberries,
   halved
2 cups seedless grapes
1 cup nectarines, unpeeled,
   sliced
½ cup kiwi fruit, peeled,
   sliced
⅓ cup freshly squeezed
   orange juice
2 tablespoons lemon juice
1½ tablespoons honey
¼ teaspoon ground ginger
⅛ teaspoon ground
   nutmeg

1. Gently toss mango, blueberries, bananas, strawberries, grapes, nectarines, and kiwi together in a large mixing bowl.
2. Stir orange juice, lemon juice, honey, ginger, and nutmeg together in a small bowl and mix well.
3. Chill fruit until needed, up to 3 hours. Just before serving, pour honey-orange sauce over fruit and toss gently to coat.

A WORD OF WISDOM

Preparing all of these fruits may be the most difficult part of this recipe. To peel ripe mangos and kiwi, slide a spoon, bottom side up, under the skin to remove it easily, without damaging the fruit.

BLACKBIRD SALT COD TOAST

On the ship known as the *Blackbird*, many leave the Wall to pursue different agendas. A hunk of salt cod and a heel of crusty bread would be common enough sights on a journey south on the narrow sea, but the commonplace can be prized as much as the rare—and anyone with Samwell Tarly's taste for food or Maester Aemon's nose for simple luxuries would find this snack a welcome distraction from the dangers in the deep. (*A Feast for Crows*, Chapter 15—Samwell)

SERVES 6–8

1 baguette of French bread
¼ cup extra-virgin olive oil
1 tablespoon kosher salt
½ pound salt cod, soaked
   for 24 hours (water
   changed 4 times), drained
1 garlic clove, peeled
⅓ cup milk
¼ cup olive oil
1 tablespoon lemon juice
Pinch nutmeg
1 teaspoon black pepper
Salt to taste

1. Preheat oven to 350°F. Slice the baguette into ¼-inch-thick rounds and lay them out on a cookie sheet. Toast them in the oven for about 5 minutes. Turn them over and toast the other side. Remove from oven and set aside.
2. Drizzle each piece of toast with olive oil and sprinkle with salt. Set aside.
3. Put the soaked and drained salt cod into a pot with water to cover. Bring the water to a simmer and poach for 10 minutes. Drain and take out any bones or skin.
4. Put the poached cod in a food processor with the garlic. Pulse a few times, then add the milk and oil through the feed tube with the machine running to make a thick purée. Stop adding the liquid if it starts to get too loose. You want a spread consistency.
5. Add the lemon juice, nutmeg, and pepper and pulse to combine. Taste and add salt if necessary.
6. Transfer the spread to an earthenware bowl and keep it warm in the oven until time to serve. Serve by spreading on the toasted bread.

A WORD OF WISDOM

Some salt cod products are presoaked and will be labeled as such. Presoaked salt cod can shave a whole day off the preparation time!

Sandor Clegane's Pickled Pigs' Feet

The Hound isn't to many people's taste—nor is his chosen wedding "gift" of pickled pigs' feet. But if the history of Westeros teaches its people anything, it's that sometimes the people and things that are seen as unwanted or beneath notice, the discarded bits and seeming mistakes, can wind up having a great and positive effect in the long run. Many who have tried this dish have been surprised by what tastes it brings to the table. (*A Storm of Swords*, Chapter 50—Arya)

MAKES 2 QUARTS

6 pigs' feet, halved
Kosher salt to taste
2 quarts vinegar
1 small red pepper, chopped
2 tablespoons grated horseradish
1 teaspoon whole black pepper
1 bay leaf

1. Scrape and scald pigs' feet. Sprinkle lightly with kosher salt. Let stand for 6 hours. Rinse well in clean water.
2. In a large pot, cook the feet in water until tender.
3. Make the vinegar stock with remaining ingredients. Bring to a boil. Pack feet into sterilized Mason jars.
4. Fill jars with boiling spiced vinegar, leaving ½-inch headspace. Clean rim and cap and tighten the band. Place jars on a rack in a pressure canner and add boiling water according to the manufacturers' instructions, usually several inches. Lock the lid securely into place. Leave weight off the vent pipe or open petcock and exhaust steam for 10 minutes. Place weight back onto vent pipe or close petcock. Canner should start to pressurize in 5–10 minutes. Once the canner has reached 10 pounds of pressure, start the timer. Process jars in pressure canner for 30 minutes at 10 pounds of pressure. Allow the pressure to return to zero on its own.
5. Let jars sit in the canner for 5–10 minutes to allow them to cool. Remove jars with a jar lifter and place them on a towel-covered counter to cool. Leave undisturbed for 12–24 hours. Check the seals and remove the screwbands.

A Word of Wisdom

This is a traditional recipe that people either love or hate. It adapts well to minor tinkering, so add spices according to your personal taste.

Ten Towers Cold Beef and Oldtown Mustard

Between two unwanted reunions and the hard journey to get there, proud Asha Greyjoy's arrival at Ten Towers is hardly comfortable. A snack of cold beef and mustard is hardly enough to fill Asha's crew or make the Kraken's Daughter relax, but it's meal enough to make old Three-Tooth smile. Cobbled together from different lands—the beef from the mainland and the mustard from Oldtown—this dish resembles the awkwardly constructed castle it is served in, a patchwork palace that is strangely emblematic of the divided nation of Westeros itself. (*A Feast for Crows*, Chapter 11—The Kraken's Daughter)

SERVES 4

2 teaspoons black peppercorns

Pinch kosher salt

1 (6-ounce) beef tenderloin filet, 1½ inches thick

1 teaspoon butter

2 tablespoons cognac plus 1 teaspoon

¼ cup heavy cream

1 ounce Stilton, Gorgonzola, Cabrales, or Roquefort cheese (optional)

4 to 5 sprigs fresh chervil

Mustard:

⅔ cup yellow mustard seeds

½ teaspoon dill weed, dried

½ teaspoon celery seed

1 teaspoon salt

2 tablespoons dry white wine

2 tablespoons white vinegar

1 tablespoon honey

Ten Towers Cold Beef and Oldtown Mustard

(CONTINUED)

1. TO PREPARE THE BEEF: Crack the peppercorns in one layer on a cutting board with the bottom of a heavy pan. Lean on it; don't hammer it. Sprinkle the salt on the filet, then press the meat into the peppercorns to coat both sides.

2. Melt the butter in a small, heavy, stainless steel sauté pan over medium-high heat until very hot. Swirl it around and let it sizzle, then brown the filet in it, 4 minutes per side.

3. Remove the filets and keep them in a warm oven while preparing the sauce. On zero heat, add 2 tablespoons of cognac to the pan and carefully ignite the alcohol with a long fireplace match. When the flames die down, turn the heat to medium and stir the liquid in the skillet, scraping up any browned bits from the bottom.

4. Add the cream and bring the sauce to a simmer. Cook and swirl until the sauce begins to thicken, maybe 3 minutes. Add the teaspoon of cognac, stir, and taste to see if you need additional salt. Return the filet to the pan, and cook it 30 seconds per side in the sauce.

5. Slice the filet and plate it. Spoon the pan sauce over it and crumble the blue cheese on top. Garnish with the sprigs of chervil. If serving to late-night guests, chill and serve with homemade Oldtown Mustard.

6. TO PREPARE MUSTARD: Using a mortar and pestle, grind the mustard seeds. You can pulverize them to a powder or leave them coarse, whichever you prefer. Place the ground seeds or powder in a bowl. Add the dry spices and the salt. Add the wine, vinegar, and honey, whisking vigorously. Depending on the fineness of the seeds (powder will take more liquid than coarse), you may need to whisk in more liquid. Taste to adjust for seasonings. If too wet, add quick-blending flour (e.g., Wondra).

A Word of Wisdom

Though it's a common condiment, mustard isn't without its own lore. Some consider it an aphrodisiac that also supports well-being. Others use it to ward off malevolent spirits.

DORAN'S FAVORITE CHICKPEA PASTE

Prince Doran Martell may be royalty, but simplicity still pleases him—especially when he is lost in his thoughts. Chickpea paste may not seem extravagant, but it is the perfect snack for a thinker looking out at the world and pondering its meaning. Reflect on life with every bite of the savory flavors of sand dunes and the famed Water Gardens. (*A Feast for Crows*, Chapter 2—The Captain of the Guards)

MAKES 2 CUPS

1 cup dried chickpeas, soaked overnight if desired, or 1 (16-ounce) can

2 cloves garlic, peeled

3 tablespoons tahini

½ teaspoon kosher salt

2–3 teaspoons toasted cumin powder (see "A Word of Wisdom")

Juice of 1 lemon, divided in half

¼ cup extra-virgin olive oil, plus a little extra for garnish

Freshly ground black pepper

Paprika and chopped parsley for garnish (optional)

Soft Flatbread from Across the Narrow Sea (Chapter 3)

DORAN'S FAVORITE CHICKPEA PASTE

(CONTINUED)

1. If using dried chickpeas, cook them in lightly salted water until very, very tender. If using canned chickpeas, drain and rinse them.
2. In a food processor, chop the garlic until it sticks to the sides of the bowl. Add chickpeas, tahini, salt, cumin, and half of the lemon juice. Process until smooth, gradually drizzling in the olive oil. (Add up to ¼ cup cold water to achieve a softer paste if desired.) Season to taste with black pepper, and additional salt and lemon juice to taste.
3. Spread onto plates and garnish with a drizzle of extra-virgin olive oil, a few drops of lemon juice, a dusting of paprika, and some chopped parsley. Serve with wedges of warm Soft Flatbread from Across the Narrow Sea, kalamata olives, and feta.

A WORD OF WISDOM

For the perfect dip, toast whole cumin seeds in a dry pan until they give off a slight smoke, and brown slightly, about 2 minutes over medium heat. Pulverize them in a coffee grinder or with a mortar and pestle. This will make your chickpea paste unforgettable. If starting with powdered cumin, just give it a quick toast in a dry pan, until it becomes highly fragrant, about 1 minute.

ROAD TO RIVERRUN APPLE CHIPS

Their towns and villages ravaged by the war between the King of the Iron Throne and the King of the North, people of the Riverlands are less and less likely to offer bread and salt to tired travelers passing though. But the Brotherhood Without Banners isn't just any band of outlaws, and the villagers it protects are happy to give what they can to the road-weary wanderers—even if meals are no more filling than a mug of ale and some dried apples. After the other crops were destroyed, apples from overlooked root cellars or salvaged from an orchard would be a precious food source for a pillaged town. That the Brotherhood is offered this snack so willingly shows the depths of the villagers' loyalty and gratitude. (*A Storm of Swords*, Chapter 17—Arya)

MAKES 2 CUPS

5 pounds fresh apples, washed and peeled (if desired)

Cinnamon and nutmeg to taste

1. Preheat oven to 150°F.
2. Slice apples into wedges. Arrange on a metal cake rack or cookie sheet. Dust with cinnamon or nutmeg.
3. Place cake rack or cookie sheet on the middle rack of the oven. If using a cookie sheet, flip the apples several times while baking to expose both sides to the heat.
4. Bake for at least 10 hours, or until fruit is leathery, flexible, and has the texture of a raisin. If you prefer a crispier texture, continue to bake for up to 10 additional hours.

A WORD OF WISDOM

There's more than one way to dry fruit. A dehydrator might be the easiest tool to use, but the sun is just as effective. Just about any warm, bright spot will do so long as your fruit is protected from wildlife and bugs, and is turned often enough for both sides to dry!

DORNISH CHEESE FLIGHT OF FANCY

As the sun sets and the air grows cool, Prince Doran does not retreat to a warm hearth. Instead, the pensive prince sits beneath an orange tree, looking out over the sea that lies in the distance, sleep escaping him as he thinks. No matter the pull of such introspective moods, it's important not to ignore the body while the mind feasts. This plate of fine cheese serves as a good snack for just such an occasion, with tempting flavors for both corporeal and spiritual senses. (*A Feast for Crows*, Chapter 2—The Captain of the Guards)

<u>SERVES 4</u>

2 ounces feta cheese

2 ounces mizithra cheese

2 ounces manouri cheese

2 ounces kefalotyri cheese

12 kalamata olives

4 fresh figs

1 walnut-size chunk of
   honeycomb

4 rounds of Soft Flatbread
   from Across the Narrow
   Sea (Chapter 3)

1. Cut the feta cheese into cubes and crumble the mizithra, manouri, and kefalotyri cheeses into bite-size chunks. Place the cheeses on a platter.
2. Arrange the kalamata olives, figs, and honeycomb on the platter.
3. Cut the flatbread into wedges and serve with the cheese.

A WORD OF WISDOM

A cheese flight is an appetizer offering a variety of cheeses meant to be tasted and compared, like a wine tasting. To some, a cheese flight simply pairs cheese selections with specific wines; others distinguish a "flight" from a "plate" by the selection of cheeses and other foods offered.

ILLYRIO'S GOOSE LIVER DROWNED IN WINE

Tyrion Lannister has feasted in many courts and castles, but to his surprise Magister Illyrio Mopatis's cooks may put the rest to shame. Delightful dishes such as Illyrio's Goose Liver Drowned in Wine convince the dwarf that he has never eaten so well before—not even in the royal court at King's Landing. With praise such as that, it may be impossible for anyone to forgo this rich pâté. (*A Dance with Dragons*, Chapter 1—Tyrion)

SERVES 6–8

1 pound goose livers

1 cup chicken broth

1 small onion, sliced

1 sprig fresh rosemary

8 cooked bacon strips, crumbled

½ cup (1 stick) unsalted butter, softened, plus 2 tablespoons unsalted butter

2 tablespoons brandy or cognac

1 tablespoon Dijon mustard

Kosher salt and freshly cracked black pepper to taste

1 quart of white wine

1. Cut goose livers in half and simmer in chicken broth in a small pot with onion and rosemary for about 15 minutes, until tender. Let cool. Reserve onion and ¼ cup of the broth. Remove leaves from the sprig of rosemary and chop fine.

2. In a food processor, combine liver, onion, ¼ cup reserved broth, chopped rosemary, crumbled bacon, ½ cup butter, cognac, and mustard. Process until smooth. Season to taste with salt and pepper.

3. Spoon the goose liver pâté into a covered container. Refrigerate overnight so flavors will blend. (Will keep 3 or 4 days in the refrigerator.)

4. Before serving, heat the wine in a large, shallow pan on medium-high. Allow to boil until reduced to 1 cup. Cut the reserved 2 tablespoons butter into thin pats and whisk them into the reduced wine to aid in thickening. Serve alongside pâté.

A WORD OF WISDOM

Serve this pâté with buttered toast points, melba or rye crackers, Soft Flatbread from Across the Narrow Sea, Winterfell Black Bread (both Chapter 3), peperoncini, dates, and figs.

FIERY VENGEANCE STUFFED PEPPERS OF DORNE

Late into the night, a strange feast is held at Sunspear. A grinning skull presides over seven courses served in honor of the Seven and the brothers of the Kingsguard. Along with soup, fish, wine, and vengeance, a plate of long green stuffed peppers tempts Princess Arianne Martell. The taste they bring would be suitable for any god's dinner table. (*A Dance with Dragons*, Chapter 38—The Watcher)

SERVES 4

½ cup shredded jack cheese

¼ cup softened cream cheese

¼ cup chopped onion

1 teaspoon ground cumin

Salt to taste

12 fresh jalapeño peppers, halved lengthwise (remove seeds for a more mild dish)

1 tablespoon extra-virgin olive oil

1. In a mixing bowl, combine the jack cheese and cream cheese with a wooden spoon until well blended.
2. Add the onion to the cheeses and stir it in gently. Stir in the cumin and season with salt to taste.
3. Spoon filling into each pepper, dividing it equally among the peppers, and place the stuffed peppers in a casserole dish. Refrigerate it at this point if serving later.
4. Preheat the oven to 350°F. Bring the stuffed peppers to room temperature if they have been refrigerated.
5. Drizzle the peppers with the olive oil. Bake for 20 to 30 minutes until cheese is melted and edges of peppers are beginning to brown. Serve warm.

A WORD OF WISDOM

Switch up the flavors in this recipe for a variety of delicious dishes. Add bacon and cilantro to this recipe for an extra savory twist. For a sweeter plate, substitute crabmeat, parsley, and goat cheese in roasted piquillo peppers for the onions, cumin, and jack cheese.

THE CHEESEMONGER'S CANDIED ONIONS

Magister Illyrio serves his clever and resourceful allies the highest Pentoshi cuisine. Candied onions work wonderfully alone as an appetizer or as a side to a larger feast. And despite such a simple recipe, this dish is sweet enough to keep the rotund cheesemonger stately and stout. (*A Dance with Dragons*, Chapter 1—Tyrion)

SERVES UP TO 40

1 bag (2 cups) peeled pearl onions

2 teaspoons sugar or brown sugar

¼ teaspoon salt

1 tablespoon butter or olive oil

1 cup cold water

1. In a heavy-bottomed skillet over medium heat, combine onions, sugar, salt, and butter with 1 cup cold water; bring to a simmer.
2. Cook gently until all water is absorbed and onions are coated in a light glaze, about 5 minutes.
3. Reduce heat to low. Cook slowly until glaze browns and onions attain golden-brown appearance, about 5 minutes more.
4. ALTERNATIVE METHOD: Once liquid is reduced to a glaze, put the entire pan in a preheated 350°F oven, and roast until browned.

A Word of Wisdom

Frozen and peeled pearl onions make this recipe very easy to make, but the sweetness and crunch of fresh ones elevates the dish in grand Pentoshi style. Use the freshest ingredients you can find—when you have the time and patience to peel for 20 minutes or so—for the best dish in the city.

PENTOSHI STINKY CHEESE PLATE

Any friend of his friend across the narrow sea is a friend of Illyrio Mopatis of Pentos. This is very fortunate for a certain Lannister who found himself in grave circumstances and in need of some hospitality—and a prodigious amount of wine. A perfect accompaniment to a good cask of strongwine, this plate of cheese simply reeks of hospitality. (*A Dance with Dragons*, Chapter 1—Tyrion)

SERVES 4

4 ounces Brie de Meaux
  cheese
4 ounces Roquefort blue
  cheese
1 French Butter pear
Handful of raspberries
¼ cup toasted hazelnuts
¼ cup toasted almonds
12 Picholine olives
¼ cup Niçoise olives
1 baguette French bread

1. Place the whole pieces of cheese on a platter.
2. Slice the pear and arrange it with the raspberries, nuts, and olives on the platter.
3. Slice the baguette and serve it with the cheese plate. Provide a cheese knife and serving fork.

A WORD OF WISDOM

Creamy Brie de Meaux has a stronger, more fermented smell than its less-specific cousins, but is known as the "King of Cheeses." Salty, crumbly Roquefort is an equally popular blue cheese made of sheep's milk with patches of aromatic green mold throughout.

BALERION FISH ROE DIP

On the stormy narrow sea, Daenerys cannot help but admire the life that dwells in the ocean waters. While the Dothraki may call it the poison water, Dany loves watching the dolphins and many forms of marine life. The sailors, the sea life, and freshly prepared Balerion Fish Roe Dip remind her of a time when she had wanted to be a sailor rather than a member of royalty. (*A Storm of Swords*, Chapter 8—Daenerys)

MAKES 2 CUPS

5 slices white bread, crusts removed

½ yellow onion

2 lemons

4 ounces tarama (cured carp or cod roe)

1 cup olive oil

1 cup mashed potatoes

1. Cut the bread and onion into chunks. Juice the lemons and discard the rinds.
2. Put all the ingredients in a food processor and blend until smooth. Serve on warm Soft Flatbread from Across the Narrow Sea (Chapter 3).

A WORD OF WISDOM

If you can't find tarama or aren't sure what it will taste like, try crabmeat or tuna in its place to make a familiar-tasting seafood spread before you attempt the real thing.

VOLANTENE HONEY SAUSAGES

South of the river Volaenia lies the eastern free city of Volantis. Known for food, illicit pleasures, and slave trade, it is in this city that Tyrion Lannister finds himself the unlikely breakfast companion of a certain knight. But rather than sulk, the Lannister Lord knows to take enjoyment where he can, and this most gratifying honey sausage offers at least some relief from the pressures and fears he otherwise feels. (*A Dance with Dragons*, Chapter 27—Tyrion)

SERVES 10

8 thickly cut slices salami
   or bologna
16 slices Winterfell Black
   Bread (Chapter 3)
8 ounces mustard pickles
4 teaspoons honey Dijon
   mustard

1. Heat the grill to hot.
2. Place the sausage slices on the hot grill and turn after 1 minute.
3. Toast the bread on the side of the grill until lightly crisped on both sides. Cut the toasted bread slices into halves and place on a serving platter.
4. Remove the sausage slices from the grill and cut into quarters. Arrange the slices of sausage on the pieces of toast. Garnish with mustard pickles and honey Dijon.

A WORD OF WISDOM

Sausage dishes like this one are a particular favorite for bars and inns. The salt and savory flavors keep drinkers thirsty—making this easy dish literally worth its salt!

BOLTON WEDDING COD CAKES

Any time two great Westerosian houses are united, feasts are elaborate, and the Lord of White Harbor would not allow a wedding to happen without serving the finest food and drink. The feast—these cod cakes included—was so disarmingly delicious that no one noticed the proverbial elephant in the room . . . except Reek (which rhymes with leek). (*A Dance with Dragons*, Chapter 37—The Prince of Winterfell)

SERVES 6

1 pound cod
2 leeks
1 red pepper
2 egg whites
Pinch of kosher salt
Fresh-cracked black
   pepper
1 tablespoon olive oil

1. Finely shred the raw fish with a fork. Dice the leeks and red pepper. Combine all the ingredients except the oil in a medium-size bowl; mix well. Form the mixture into small oval patties.
2. Heat the oil in a medium-size sauté pan. Place the cakes in the pan and loosely cover with the lid. Sauté the cakes for 4 to 6 minutes on each side. Drain on a rack covered with paper towels; serve immediately.

A WORD OF WISDOM

If you don't have cod on hand, feel free to substitute a similar whitefish like haddock, halibut, pollock, or sole.

The Hedge Knight's Salt Beef Salami

A century before Ned Stark serves as the Hand of the King, the squire called Dunk finds his life changed. As he makes his way to Ashford, he ponders his station in life, camping rather than staying in a grand hall, eating salt beef rather than capons and suckling pigs. It's no wonder that wandering knights and travelers kept salt beef as a staple: made correctly, salami can keep for years at room temperature! Since this is not a long-curing variety, this homemade version should be kept in the refrigerator. (*The Hedge Knight*)

MAKES 6–8 SMALL ROLLS

5 pounds ground beef

5 teaspoons salt

5 hot peppercorns, crushed

2 teaspoons garlic powder

1½ teaspoons mustard
   seed

2½ teaspoons hickory-
   smoked salt

2 teaspoons onion powder

5 teaspoons curing salt

2 teaspoons ground
   caraway seed

1. Combine all ingredients in a large bowl; knead 5 minutes. Cover tightly with plastic wrap; refrigerate 24 hours.
2. Knead mixture 5 minutes. Cover tightly with plastic wrap; refrigerate another 24 hours.
3. Knead 5 minutes; form into 6–8 small rolls. Place on a broiler pan; bake 8 hours at 150°F, turning every hour. Turn oven off; let salami cool on broiler rack still in the oven until it reaches room temperature.
4. Wrap tightly in plastic wrap. Refrigerate and slice. Serve on crackers or bread.

A Word of Wisdom

You may substitute onion salt or garlic salt for the powder in this recipe if you like your salami on the salty side. For the recipe to succeed, you must always use curing salt or quick-cure salt.

GHISCARI SPICED HONEYED LOCUSTS

Strong Belwas will agree that this Ghiscari specialty is of such taste that it is nearly worth dying for. Any dish that so perfectly balances honey sweetness with the savory fire of Free City spices is nothing short of tantalizing, and the preparation of such a meal is an accomplishment to take pride in. People who try this dish shouldn't be surprised to find out that one bite isn't enough! (*A Dance with Dragons*, Chapter 52—Daenerys)

SERVES 10

2 tablespoons honey

3 tablespoons lime juice

1 teaspoon grated lime zest

¼ cup soy sauce

½ cup vegetable oil, divided

2 tablespoons grated gingerroot

1 green onion, trimmed and thinly sliced

½ teaspoon ground cumin

½ teaspoon coriander

¼ cup chopped cilantro

2 teaspoons cornstarch

20 locusts or large grasshoppers, legs and wings removed

1 clove garlic, minced

1 slice gingerroot, minced

3 cups packaged fresh stir-fry vegetable mix

Salt to taste

Sugar to taste

GHISCARI SPICED HONEYED LOCUSTS
(CONTINUED)

1. TO MAKE SPICED HONEY MARINADE, combine the honey, lime juice, lime zest, and soy sauce in a bowl. Slowly whisk in ¼ cup of the oil. Stir in grated gingerroot, onion, cumin, coriander, cilantro, and cornstarch. Place locusts in liquid and marinate for 30 minutes.

2. Heat a wok or skillet over medium-high heat until it is nearly smoking. Add 2 tablespoons oil. When the oil is hot, add the garlic. Stir-fry until it is aromatic, then add the locusts. Stir and toss the locusts for 3 to 4 minutes, adding 1–2 tablespoons of marinade if they seem to be drying out. Stir-fry until locusts are just turning golden brown. Remove the locusts from the pan. Drain in a colander or on paper towels.

3. Add 2 tablespoons oil to the wok or skillet. When the oil is hot, add the minced gingerroot. Stir-fry until aromatic, then add the vegetables. Stir-fry for 1 to 2 minutes, until the vegetables are tender but still crisp. Stir in salt and sugar while stir-frying the vegetables, if desired. Add 1 to 2 tablespoons of marinade if the vegetables are drying out during stir-frying.

4. Add ½ cup of marinade and bring to a boil. Add the locusts back into the pan. Stir-fry for 2 more minutes to heat through and thoroughly cook the locusts. Serve hot.

A WORD OF WISDOM

If you prefer a more mundane meat in your stir-fry, substitute two chicken breasts for the locusts. The Ghiscari would prefer dog or camel, but the sweet and spicy sauce is very versatile.

THE QUEENMAKER'S STUFFED DATES

Beneath the sun that basks over Dorne, a motley group gathers. Garin of the Greenblood orphans, Drey Dalt, Spotted Sylva Santagar, and Ser Gerold Dayne the Darkstar discuss plans of great import while Arianne considers their loyalty and her own agenda. The conspirators share this Stuffed Date dish, a perfect treat for those who present one face on the outside and prove to have different intentions. (*A Feast for Crows*, Chapter 21—The Queenmaker)

SERVES 6

12 large Medjool dates
8 ounces mascarpone
   cheese, at room
   temperature
½ cup whole almonds
1 cup confectioners' sugar

1. Cut a slit on one side of each date and remove the pit.
2. Using a pastry bag, carefully fill each date with about 2 teaspoons of mascarpone. Add an almond on top of each.
3. Place the confectioners' sugar in a bowl. Roll the underside of the dates in the confectioners' sugar.

A WORD OF WISDOM

These treats are also fine desserts to accompany coffee, tea, or lemonsweet, and they are a simple and sweet addition to a fine cheese plate.

CHAPTER 3

Something off the Sideboard:
Sides and Bread

F inding a table in the lands of the Seven Kingdoms and beyond that does not boast a side dish or bread can be a challenge. A smaller dish with the right taste can act as a perfect mouthwatering beginning to a fine dinner, preparing the tastes buds for fuller, heartier plates yet to come. And certain types of bread add a nice flavor to things such as soups and stews, able to soak it up and fill the stomach even more.

There is also the interesting fact that simple vegetables and breads are a unifying factor in the Seven Kingdoms. Whatever banners they belong to, whatever class their families fall into, all people in all stations of life enjoy these dishes. Beggars breaking bread can imagine that what a king is enjoying at his own dinner table is not too different from the scraps they're given.

BENJEN'S ROASTED ONIONS DIPPED IN GRAVY

Brothers of the Night's Watch give up the right to have children, and put aside family and political loyalties. Despite this, Benjen Stark never truly leaves his family behind. After a long journey from the Wall, he is happy to sit in his brother Eddard's hall and looks kindly on his nieces and nephews, even the bastard Jon Snow. Benjen and Jon share a conversation and a simple plate of roasted onions—a taste of home and hearth they may both miss in the coming days. (*A Game of Thrones*, Chapter 5—Jon)

SERVES 4

4 large sweet onions, all the
   same size
2 tablespoons drippings
   from roast meat of
   your choice, or more if
   available
¼ cup all-purpose flour
2 cups milk or cream

1. Heat oven to 350°F. Trim the visible roots from the onions, but leave the skins on and the tops untrimmed. Place the onions root-end down in a baking dish. Roast in center of oven until onions are very soft, and give easily to gentle pressure. They take between 60 and 90 minutes, depending on the size of the onions.

2. Prepare gravy while onions are roasting. Heat meat drippings in a pan on medium-high. Carefully whisk 1 tablespoon of the flour into pan. Cook slowly, constantly stirring with whisk, until drippings have thickened and flour is golden brown.

3. Slowly add any remaining drippings and flour to pan, stirring constantly. When flour is completely dissolved, stir in milk or cream. You may want to use more or less cream than recommended to reach your desired consistency.

4. When onions are very soft, remove from the oven. Peel the outer skin, but leave on the caramelized outer layers, which add extra flavor. Serve dressed generously with gravy.

A WORD OF WISDOM

If you are using large onions, cut them into thirds so they roast evenly. Otherwise, keep the onions in halves. Rough chopped onions might roast quickly and do their job in a pot roast, but these onions need to be able to stand on their own!

THE LORD COMMANDER'S TURNIPS
SOAKED IN BUTTER

The night he is to take the Night Watch's vow, Jon Snow's mouth waters with anticipation over the special meal Three-Finger Hobb prepares for the newest brothers. These turnips, straight from the Old Bear's table, are a great accompaniment to roast meat and a roaring fire. Serve them with the Castle Black Rack of Lamb (Chapter 5) for the full flavor of the crows' celebration. (*A Game of Thrones*, Chapter 19—Jon)

SERVES 4

1½ pounds turnips and
  rutabagas, peeled
2 tablespoons butter
1 tablespoon chopped
  parsley
2 teaspoons chopped
  chervil or tarragon
2 tablespoons chopped
  chives
1 clove garlic, finely
  chopped
Kosher salt and black
  pepper
½ cup fresh bread crumbs
  browned in 1 tablespoon
  olive oil or butter

1. Cook the turnips and rutabagas separately in salted water until they're al dente (tender, but firm—approximately 10 minutes for turnips, 20 minutes for rutabagas); drain.
2. In a large skillet over medium heat, melt the butter. Add the turnips and rutabagas, and cook over medium-high flame until golden brown. Add herbs, garlic, salt, and pepper, and toss to coat.
3. Serve topped with bread crumbs.

A Word of Wisdom
Rutabagas and turnips have a naturally buttery flavor, especially when young and fresh in the autumn. Both would be common sights in cold storage throughout the Seven Kingdoms.

Mord's Boiled Beans

A simple dish, boiled beans are still a satisfying treat and can be eaten alone as a filling snack or as something to whet the appetite for a larger meal. Upon finding himself in a bad situation (not the first or last time for him), Tyrion Lannister knows there's a way out if he can just think of one. And who can truly think on an empty stomach? It might not be his first choice, but a plate of beans from Mord seems to be enough to help him concoct a plan. (*A Game of Thrones*, Chapter 38—Tyrion)

SERVES 6

1½ cups pigeon peas, soaked overnight, rinsed and drained

1 tablespoon olive oil

1 small Spanish onion, chopped

⅓ green pepper, chopped

2 cloves garlic, minced

2 bay leaves

1½ teaspoons salt

¼ teaspoon fresh ground black pepper

¼ cup chopped fresh thyme or 1 tablespoon dried

1 medium tomato, seeded, chopped

1. Simmer pigeon peas in 4 cups water for 1 hour, until tender. Meanwhile, heat the olive oil in a 10-inch skillet, then add onion, green pepper, garlic, bay leaves, salt, pepper, and thyme, and sauté until onion is translucent (about 5 minutes). Add chopped tomato and cook 2 minutes more.

2. Add the vegetables to the beans and cook 45 minutes more, until beans are very soft. Serve with white or yellow rice.

A Word of Wisdom

Dried beans absorb a great deal of water when soaked and will swell to as much as 150 percent of their original size. The beans will cook more quickly this way than if you just use dried beans straight from the bag. Never cook them in the soaking water.

Golden Lions' Spiced Squash

The Lannisters savor joys and pleasures (to a fault, some would say). Whether they overindulge or not, their tastes can't be faulted or questioned. During a celebratory feast, Tyrion completes his repast with this spiced squash dish. Warm and comforting, it mirrors the new home honored by the royal spread, but it also nods at his new occupation with an undeniable richness. (*A Clash of Kings*, Chapter 8—Tyrion)

SERVES 8

1 medium butternut
  squash (2–3 pounds)
2 tablespoons ground
  cumin
2 tablespoons olive oil
Salt and coarsely ground
  black pepper
1 tablespoon roughly
  chopped Italian (flat-
  leaf) parsley

1. Cut the butternut in two, crosswise, just above the bulbous bottom. Place the cut side of the cylindrical barrel down on a cutting board, and peel it with a knife or potato peeler, removing all rind. Repeat with the bottom part, then cut bottom in half and remove seeds.
2. Dice squash into 1-inch chunks. In a large mixing bowl, toss squash with cumin, oil, salt, and pepper.
3. Spread into a single layer on a doubled baking sheet, and roast in a 375°F oven for 40 minutes, turning after 25 minutes, until browned and tender. Serve sprinkled with chopped parsley.

A Word of Wisdom

Want the most squash with the fewest seeds? Choose butternuts with a large cylindrical barrel, and small bulbous bottom.

Arya's Sweetcorn Eaten on the Cob

As hard as traveling on the road was, and as difficult as her life became, Arya is still able to find some pleasure and joy in the simple eating of sweetcorn on the cob. This food is so simple to prepare, yet it's a delicious addition to almost any meal. It offers a few minutes of simple pleasure as the young girl embarks on a journey that will twist and turn in ways no one could have predicted. (*A Clash of Kings*, Chapter 9—Arya)

SERVES 8–12

8–12 ears of corn
½ cup (1 stick) unsalted
   butter, melted

1. Set the grill on medium-high.
2. Remove the husks and silk from the corn. Presoak the corn in a bowl of water for 10 to 20 minutes. Paint the corn with butter.
3. Grill for about 4 minutes per side, turning often and adding butter. Serve with more butter, salt, and pepper.

A Word of Wisdom

Some people prefer to wrap the corn in aluminum foil with a pat of butter or a cube of ice, but putting it directly on the grill gives it a lovely, rustic flavor.

LANNISTER RED FENNEL DELIGHT

Southron salads (see Chapter 4) aren't the only home for the savory flavor of fennel. Sausage-stuffed fennel, a fine side dish likely to be found on the table of a Lannister, gives the favorite herb a little flair and is inspired by fennel-filled salad and Hand of the King's Oxtail Soup (Chapter 4) served in the Tower of the Hand. And besides, Tyrion would never argue with having more options and resources at his disposal. (*A Clash of Kings*, Chapter 44—Tyrion)

SERVES 10

3¾ pounds pork or ox
¾–1½ pounds pork or ox fat
1½ bulb garlic
¼ cup plus 2 tablespoons fennel seeds
3 tablespoons dried basil
3 tablespoons dried oregano
Freshly cracked black pepper to taste
Kosher salt to taste
5 large bulbs fennel
1 tablespoon olive oil

1. Grind the meat and fat separately. Keep chilled. Peel and mince the garlic.
2. Mix together all the ingredients except fennel bulbs and olive oil in a chilled bowl with chilled utensils. If using an electric mixer, be sure not to overblend the meat and fat. Keep sausage mix chilled while preparing fennel.
3. Clean and trim the fennel bulbs (cut off the stalks; use only the bottom bulb). Boil until al dente. Remove, drain, and let cool.
4. Preheat oven to 375°F. Grease a large baking dish with the oil. Carefully slice the fennel bulbs in half; keep the base (root piece) intact on each half. This should aid in keeping the "leaves" together.
5. Carefully stuff each leaf layer with the sausage mixture.
6. Place each stuffed half in the prepared baking dish cut-side down. Cover and bake for 45 minutes. Uncover and bake 15 minutes longer.
7. Drain off excess fat. Serve hot.

A WORD OF WISDOM

Besides being a favorite for gourmet salads and sandwiches, fennel seeds are a popular sausage ingredient, making it a logical pairing with ground meats in almost any form.

JEYNE'S STEWED ONIONS AND LEEKS

With Queen Jeyne so attentive, Robb need never go hungry, even when he's busy making plans for his next attack on the Lannisters. A perfect side dish for a meal of roasted meat, this recipe should bring any young warrior back to his senses with the overwhelming taste of a hearth-cooked meal and a dash of love from a pretty young spouse. (*A Storm of Swords*, Chapter 20—Catelyn)

<u>SERVES 4</u>

5 black peppercorns
5 parsley stems
1 bay leaf
1 onion, halved, plus 2
   onions, whole and peeled
2 carrots, thinly sliced
1 rib celery, sliced
2 teaspoons salt
2 leeks, cleaned, halved
   lengthwise
1 tablespoon extra-virgin
   olive oil
Chopped chives or parsley

1. Combine peppercorns, parsley stems, bay leaf, halved onion, carrots, and celery in a nonreactive pot with 3 quarts of water and 2 teaspoons salt. Bring to a boil; lower to a simmer. Add the whole onions and leeks; simmer very gently for 15 to 20 minutes, until leeks are very tender.
2. Remove leeks and whole onions from the broth; arrange them cut-side up on a platter. Drizzle with olive oil and sprinkle with chives.

WORD OF WISDOM

Braised leeks are a juicy, light side dish perfect with spicy dishes and fried foods as well as with meat. Use the broth left from cooking the leeks in soups, stews, and risottos. Remember to wash leeks very well, twice even, as they often contain lots of sandy grit.

Cersei's Buttered Beets

Celebrating a victory, Cersei toasts her "true friends" and promises, as always, that the Lannisters will pay their debts (one way or another). As those gathered rejoice and celebrate, the queen feasts on the almost overpowering sweetness of White Harbor Hippocras (Chapter 6) and buttered beets—as well as on her guests' toadying. Full of red wine, vegetables, and meat, Cersei's meal couldn't be more representative of the blood she'll have on her hands if all goes to plan. (*A Feast for Crows*, Chapter 24—Cersei)

SERVES 8

2 pounds beets (about 8, tangerine-size), peeled, cut into 1-inch wedges

1 tablespoon olive oil

¼ teaspoon ground cinnamon

¼ teaspoon salt

2 tablespoons butter

Chopped Italian parsley (optional)

1. Heat oven to 350°F.
2. Toss beets with olive oil, cinnamon, and salt. Spread into a single layer on a baking sheet (preferably nonstick).
3. Roast on the middle rack of the oven until tender, about 1 hour, turning once after 30 minutes.
4. Melt butter and drizzle over beets on serving dish. If desired, serve sprinkled with chopped parsley.

A Word of Wisdom

The best part of beets—the flavorful, nutrient-rich juice—is water-soluble, and if you aren't careful, you'll lose it when you cook them! Lock in the sweetness, color, and nutrition by cooking them in their skins. A few drops of red wine vinegar will help seal in beet juices if you're boiling them. Beets can also be baked whole, like potatoes, and then peeled and sliced.

Braavosian Frog Legs

As Arya Stark is told, the waters that surround the nation of Braavos are host to marine life of all sorts, as well as frogs, turtles, and shellfish. Frog legs make a tasty treat for the people of Braavos quick enough to catch the little critters (as any trained water dancer should be able to) and would serve well as appetizers at a party or side dishes for a greater feast. (*A Feast for Crows*, Chapter 22—Arya)

SERVES 4–5

2 pounds frog legs
Salt and pepper to taste
1 cup flour
8 tablespoons (1 stick) butter
2 cloves garlic, minced
1 lemon
1 cup dry white wine
1 tablespoon capers (optional)
¼ cup fresh Italian parsley, chopped
1 loaf crusty bread

1. Season the frog legs with salt and pepper and lightly dredge in flour. Place on a baking tray.
2. Melt the butter in a skillet and sauté frog legs over medium-high heat until golden brown and tender, about 6 to 8 minutes.
3. Add the garlic to the butter in the pan and cook for a minute.
4. Squeeze lemon juice over the legs. Add wine and capers (optional). Simmer for a few minutes more. Sprinkle with chopped parsley.
5. Serve with crusty bread and a glass of the dry white wine.

A Word of Wisdom

To embellish this classic recipe, try adding fire-roasted red peppers or tomatoes for an extra southron flair.

Bolton Savory Stuffed Winter Squash

Lord Roose Bolton serves this northern specialty at a wedding feast. Packed with delicious onions, mushrooms, nuts, and herbs, this posh dish with its sweet taste juxtaposes the cold and sometimes cruel nature of Bolton himself, a nature that does not crack even at such a celebration. Though he may not appreciate its flavor—and irony—that shouldn't stop others from doing so. (*A Dance with Dragons*, Chapter 37—The Prince of Winterfell)

SERVES 4

2 acorn squash

1 teaspoon garlic powder

½ teaspoon salt

2 tablespoons butter

2 ribs celery, chopped

1 onion, diced

½ cup sliced mushrooms

¼ cup chopped walnuts

1 tablespoon soy sauce

1 teaspoon parsley

½ teaspoon thyme

½ teaspoon sage

Salt and pepper to taste

½ cup grated Swiss cheese

1. Preheat oven to 350°F. Chop the squash in half lengthwise and scrape out any stringy bits and seeds.
2. Dust squash with garlic powder and salt, then place cut-side down on a baking sheet and bake for 30 minutes or until almost soft; remove from oven.
3. In a large skillet, melt the butter. Add the celery, onion, and mushrooms and cook over medium heat until soft, about 4–5 minutes.
4. Add walnuts, soy sauce, parsley, thyme, and sage, stirring to combine well, and season generously with salt and pepper. Heat for another 1 or 2 minutes until fragrant.
5. Fill squash with mushroom mixture and sprinkle with cheese. Bake another 5–10 minutes until squash is soft.

A Word of Wisdom

This recipe combines all the flavors of fall baked into one nutritious dish. Use fresh herbs if you have them, and breathe deep to savor the impossibly magical aromas coming from your kitchen.

Pentoshi Mushrooms in Butter and Garlic

Even when he fears that he is being led into a trap and that the dish before him may be poisoned, Tyrion cannot help but acknowledge his desire for just a taste of it. The mushrooms before him glistening with butter and smelling of garlic make his mouth water, and it's no wonder. Poisoned or not, this savory dish would tempt just about anyone.
(*A Dance with Dragons,* Chapter 1—Tyrion)

SERVES 4

4 large portobello mushrooms with stems

6 tablespoons (¾ stick) unsalted butter, divided

4 large white onions, finely chopped

10 cloves garlic, finely chopped

1 cup arborio rice

5 cups vegetable stock or water

2 tablespoons grated imported Parmesan cheese, preferably Parmigiano-Reggiano

Salt and freshly ground pepper to taste

1 bunch scallions, finely chopped

Scented olive oil, such as truffle oil, garlic oil, or herb oil (or very good extra-virgin olive oil)

PENTOSHI MUSHROOMS IN BUTTER AND GARLIC
(CONTINUED)

1. Finely chop the stems of the mushrooms. Set the caps aside. In a large saucepan, melt 5 tablespoons of the butter, and sauté the onions and garlic over medium heat until translucent, about 2 minutes. Add the chopped mushroom stems, and sauté a minute longer. Season with salt.

2. Add the rice. Stir well to coat, then add 1 cup of stock and stir until the liquid is mostly absorbed. Add another cup of stock, stirring constantly, and allow the rice to absorb it. Continue adding stock cup by cup, until all liquid is used and rice is tender, but still a little firm to the bite in the middle (about 25 minutes). Stir in remaining 1 tablespoon butter and the cheese, and season to taste with salt and freshly ground black pepper. Set aside.

3. Slice the portobello caps paper-thin. Divide risotto into 4 bowls, immediately sprinkle with the shaved portobellos, and garnish with scallions and a drizzle (about 2 teaspoons) of truffle oil (or other flavored oil).

A WORD OF WISDOM

Need to know your mushrooms? Creminis are just young portobellos; both are nutty, and gourmand favorites. Fluted oyster mushrooms have a more subtle flavor. Any young mushroom can be called a button, but chefs usually reserve the name for the white button variety. White mushrooms are simply button mushrooms with the caps fully opened.

THE DEAD MAN'S ROASTED VEGETABLES

The perfect side for a dish of wild game, roasted vegetables are a common Westerosian addition to many meals. But for Ser Davos, who finds himself yet again in captivity and presumed dead, they are much more than common; they are a blessing. For a taste of the finest dungeon fare in the Seven Kingdoms, plate these with spiced mutton and fresh Westrosian Barley Bread (this chapter). (*A Dance with Dragons*, Chapter 29—Davos)

SERVES 4

3 carrots, chopped

2 small turnips, chopped

2 sweet potatoes, chopped

2 tablespoons olive oil

Salt and pepper to taste

⅓ cup maple syrup

2 tablespoons Dijon
   mustard

1 tablespoon balsamic
   vinegar

½ teaspoon hot sauce

1. Preheat oven to 400°F.
2. On a large baking sheet, spread out chopped carrots, turnips, and sweet potatoes. Drizzle with olive oil and season generously with salt and pepper. Roast for 40 minutes, tossing once.
3. In a small bowl, whisk together maple syrup, Dijon mustard, balsamic vinegar, and hot sauce.
4. Transfer the roasted vegetables to a large bowl and toss well with the maple mixture. Add more salt and pepper to taste.

A Word of Wisdom

Get creative with the vegetables you choose to roast and glaze with this recipe: Brussels sprouts, beets, parsnips, baby new potatoes, squash, and daikon radish would all be lovely with this tangy-sweet glaze.

Illyrio's Buttered Parsnip Purée

As if Illyrio's Goose Liver Drowned in Wine, the Cheesemonger's Candied Onions (both in Chapter 2), and Pentoshi Mushrooms in Butter and Garlic (in this chapter) aren't enough elegance for one table, the Pentoshi magister's chefs perfect the opulent spread with a deceptively simple purée. Like the little birds and mice that helped establish Illyrio's wealth and power, this sweet and creamy dish could easily go unnoticed when present, but when absent might be missed sorely. (*A Dance with Dragons*, Chapter 1—Tyrion)

SERVES 6

2 pounds parsnips
½ cup milk
8 tablespoons (1 stick) unsalted butter
Salt

1. Peel the parsnips and boil in salted water. Cook until very tender, about 10 to 15 minutes. Drain in a colander. While the parsnips are draining, heat the milk in a small pot.
2. Combine the parsnips and milk in a food processor or blender. With the motor going, gradually add the butter, making sure it is well mixed, and the purée is very smooth. Season lightly with salt.

A Word of Wisdom

Some farmers leave some parsnips in the ground over winter. The frozen earth turns starches into sugars, so when the ground thaws and the parsnips are dug up, the roots are super-sweet.

Winterfell Black Bread

In the halls of Winterfell, black bread is easy to find. Of course, bread can be found in many lands and nations, but the black bread of the North is fitting for its inhabitants. It possesses a darker color, higher fiber, and stronger flavor than other breads. It's denser as well, implying a great inner strength. Such food seems to symbolize the soul of the Stark family: gritty and stronger than anyone gives them credit for, with hidden resources that emerge when needed. Flavorful and healthy, it's both a treat and practical nourishment. (*A Game of Thrones*, Chapter 5—Jon)

MAKES 1 LOAF

⅔ cup warm water

1¾ teaspoons active dry yeast (1 package)

3 tablespoons molasses

2 teaspoons canola oil

1 cup medium rye flour

1 teaspoon kosher salt

1 tablespoon caraway seeds, toasted and ground

2–3 cups bread flour

1 tablespoon honey

1 tablespoon strong coffee

WINTERFELL BLACK BREAD

(CONTINUED)

1. In a large bowl, combine water, yeast, and 1 tablespoon of the molasses. Stir to dissolve and let stand until foamy, about 10 minutes.

2. Add remaining molasses, oil, and rye flour; stir to combine. Add salt, caraway, and enough bread flour to create a firm dough. Add flour only to reduce stickiness. Turn out onto a floured surface and knead 5–8 minutes. Return to bowl, dust the top with flour, and cover with a damp cloth or plastic wrap. Rise at room temperature until doubled in volume, about 2 hours.

3. Coat a 9" × 5" loaf pan with pan spray and line the bottom and short sides with a strip of parchment. (If you don't have pan spray and parchment, grease the bottom and sides of pan with vegetable shortening.) Turn risen dough onto a floured surface and shape into an oblong loaf. Place into prepared pan and set aside to proof for 30 minutes, or until dough rises above the pan. Preheat oven to 350°F.

4. Combine honey and coffee; brush gently onto the surface of risen dough. Bake until golden brown and hollow sounding, about 30–40 minutes. Cool 10 minutes, remove from pan, and cool completely on a rack.

A WORD OF WISDOM

This dough is commonly baked in loaf pans that are short in height and long in length. Slices of these mini loaves make the perfect base for appetizers like Blackbird Salt Cod Toast, Illyrio's Goose Liver Drowned in Wine, and Desperate Travelers' Acorn Paste (all in Chapter 2).

INN AT THE CROSSROADS 7-GRAIN LOAF

Though she made Winterfell her home and became a mother to a family of children that respect the old gods, Catelyn Tully originally hailed from Riverrun, where they practice the Faith of the Seven. But after tragedy and conspiracy, she finds herself crossing her father's territories of the Riverlands and stops at the Inn at the Crossroads. Her thoughts drift to her childhood and those around her who worship the Seven. This 7-Grain Loaf might be a familiar flavor for such a busy inn—and would reflect the innkeep's faith as well as her patrons'. (*A Game of Thrones*, Chapter 28—Catelyn)

MAKES 2 LOAVES

1 cup warm water

1 tablespoon honey

1¾ teaspoons active dry yeast (1 package)

½ cup buttermilk

2 eggs

1 cup 7-grain cereal (see "A Word of Wisdom")

1 cup whole wheat flour

1½ teaspoons kosher salt

2–3 cups bread flour

2 tablespoons cornmeal

1 tablespoon olive oil

INN AT THE CROSSROADS 7-GRAIN LOAF

(CONTINUED)

1. In a large bowl, combine water, honey, and yeast. Stir to dissolve and let stand until foamy, about 10 minutes.

2. Add buttermilk, eggs, 7-grain cereal, and whole wheat flour; stir to combine. Add salt and enough bread flour to create a firm dough. Add flour only to reduce stickiness. Turn out onto a floured surface and knead 8–10 minutes. Return to bowl, dust the top with flour, and cover with a damp cloth or plastic wrap. Rise at room temperature until doubled in volume, about 2 hours.

3. Line a baking sheet with parchment or lightly grease the sheet. Sprinkle sheet with cornmeal. Turn risen dough onto a floured surface, divide into 2 equal portions, and shape into round loaves. Place onto prepared pan and set aside to proof for 30 minutes. Preheat oven to 375°F.

4. Brush the top of the risen loaves with olive oil. Using a serrated knife, slice a few lines into the surface of the dough, about ½-inch deep. Place a pan of cold water at the bottom of the oven to create steam. Bake until golden brown and hollow sounding, about 30–40 minutes. Cool completely on a rack before serving.

A WORD OF WISDOM

Homemade 7-grain cereal is easy to make. For 1 cup, combine 2 tablespoons each of rolled oats, brown rice, rye groats, cracked wheat, buckwheat, barley, and spelt. Add 1 tablespoon each of flax and sesame seeds for good measure, then coarsely grind the whole mixture in a food processor or coffee grinder.

WESTEROSIAN BARLEY BREAD

Barley can be found in several parts of Westeros—from the Reach to the Vale—and is traded to northmen like Yoren when they travel to southern cities. Barley can often be found at various meals, in bread and in stew. The nutty smell of a freshly baked loaf of this rustic bread would be welcome in any inn, tavern, cottage, or keep. (*A Clash of Kings*, Chapter 9—Arya)

MAKES 3 LOAVES

1 cup wheat berries

½ cup spelt groats

¼ cup barley groats

2 tablespoons whole millet

2 tablespoons dried green lentils

1 tablespoon dried white beans

1 tablespoon dried red beans

1 tablespoon dried black beans

½ cup cracked wheat

1½ cups boiling water

2 cups warm water

½ cup honey

1¾ teaspoons active dry yeast (1 package)

¼ cup olive oil

1 teaspoon kosher salt

WESTEROSIAN BARLEY BREAD

(CONTINUED)

1. In a large bowl, stir together the whole grains and beans (first 9 ingredients), then grind to a fine powder, using a flour mill, coffee grinder, or food processor. Cover with boiling water and set aside for 30 minutes to soften.

2. In another large bowl, combine warm water, 1 tablespoon of the honey, and yeast. Stir to dissolve and let stand until foamy, about 10 minutes.

3. Add to the yeast mixture the remaining honey, oil, ground grain mixture, and salt. Stir to combine, and beat 8–10 minutes. The finished batter will be lumpier and thinner than traditional bread dough. Dust the top with flour, cover with a damp cloth or plastic wrap, and rise at room temperature until doubled in volume, about 2 hours.

4. Coat three 9" × 5" loaf pans with pan spray, and line the bottom and short sides of each pan with a strip of parchment. (If you don't have pan spray and parchment, grease the bottom and sides of pans with vegetable shortening.) Stir risen batter and divide evenly among prepared pans. Cover and set aside to proof for 30 minutes, or until dough rises to the top of the pans. Preheat oven to 350°F.

5. Bake risen loaves until golden brown and hollow sounding, about 45–50 minutes. Cool 10 minutes, remove from pans, and cool completely on a rack.

A WORD OF WISDOM

Barley is a favorite grain for malting. Bakers use barley malt as a sweetener and brewers swear by it when making beer. Pairing this with a brew like Direwolf Ale or Merman's Black Stout (both in Chapter 6) would be a perfect match.

Black Brothers' Oat Bread

Warm, thick slices of this breakfast bread would thaw any ranger to the core. Whether you're eating it with a pat of butter or covering it with Northmen's Soft-Boiled Eggs and Bacon (Chapter 1), the Black Brothers' Oat Bread can even fill Qhorin Halfhand's stomach. (*A Clash of Kings*, Chapter 43—Jon)

MAKES 2 LOAVES

2½ cups boiling water

1¾ cups steel-cut oats

1 cup raisins

1 tablespoon plus 1 pinch kosher salt

3 tablespoons butter

½ cup warm milk

3 tablespoons brown sugar

1¾ teaspoons active dry yeast (1 package)

1 cup whole wheat flour

4–6 cups bread flour

¼ cup cornmeal

1 large egg

1 cup rolled oats (not quick cooking)

BLACK BROTHERS' OAT BREAD

(CONTINUED)

1. In a large bowl, combine water, steel-cut oats, raisins, 1 tablespoon salt, and butter. Stir together, then let stand 30–45 minutes, until oats have softened. Set aside.

2. In another large bowl, combine milk, brown sugar, and yeast. Stir to dissolve and let stand until foamy, about 10 minutes.

3. Add whole wheat flour and oat mixture; stir to combine. Add enough bread flour to create a firm dough. Add flour only to reduce stickiness. Turn out onto a floured surface and knead 8–10 minutes. Return to bowl, dust the top with flour, and cover with a damp cloth or plastic wrap. Rise at room temperature until doubled in volume, about 1 hour.

4. Line a baking sheet with parchment or grease the sheet lightly. Sprinkle sheet with cornmeal. Turn risen dough onto a floured surface, divide into 2 equal portions, and shape into oblong loaves. Place onto prepared pan, seam-side down. Dust with flour, cover loosely with plastic wrap, and set aside to proof for 30 minutes. Preheat oven to 375°F.

5. Whisk egg with a pinch of salt and brush across the surface of risen loaves. Sprinkle liberally with rolled oats, and using a serrated knife, cut decorative slash marks into the surface of the dough, about ½-inch deep. Place a pan of cold water at the bottom of the oven to create steam, and bake until golden brown and hollow sounding, about 30–40 minutes. Cool completely on a rack before serving.

A WORD OF WISDOM

Oats boast so much protein that they are considered one of the most nutritious grains. The Night Watch would likely keep several oat varieties on hand for their culinary needs, including groats, steel-cut, and rolled.

Umma's Morning Loaf

Blind Beth sees the stars in her dreams, but during the day the world is black. Even a task as simple as getting dressed and going to breakfast in the morning becomes a worthwhile practice session, training her senses so she may function without sight. The smell of Umma's morning loaf is a beacon in the dark for her, a scent to follow to the promise of nourishment and the day's true beginning. (*A Dance with Dragons*, Chapter 45—The Blind Girl)

MAKES 2 LOAVES

1 cup warm water

3 tablespoons honey

1¾ teaspoons active dry yeast (1 package)

3 eggs

¼ cup olive oil, plus more as needed for tops of loaves

2 cups fresh or frozen and thawed corn kernels

1 cup scallions, finely chopped

1½ cups cornmeal

½ cup whole wheat flour

¾ teaspoon kosher salt

3–4 cups bread flour

¼ cup cornmeal

Umma's Morning Loaf

(CONTINUED)

1. In a large bowl, combine water, honey, and yeast. Stir to dissolve and let stand until foamy, about 10 minutes.
2. Add eggs, ¼ cup oil, corn, scallions, cornmeal, and whole wheat flour; stir to combine. Add salt and enough bread flour to create a firm dough. Add flour only to reduce stickiness. Turn out onto a floured surface and knead 8–10 minutes. Return to bowl, dust the top with flour, and cover with a damp cloth or plastic wrap. Rise at room temperature until doubled in volume, about 2 hours.
3. Coat two 9" × 5" loaf pans with pan spray, and dust thoroughly with cornmeal. Turn risen dough onto a floured surface, divide into 2 equal portions, and shape into oblong loaves. Place into prepared pans seam-side down. Cover loosely with plastic wrap and set aside to proof for 30 minutes, or until dough rises above the pans. Preheat oven to 375°F.

4. Brush olive oil gently onto the surface of the risen dough and sprinkle lightly with cornmeal. Bake until golden brown and hollow sounding, about 30–40 minutes. Cool 10 minutes, remove from pans, and cool completely on a rack.

A Word of Wisdom

Cornmeal gives this bread a lovely, sweet flavor and a hearty texture. Any type of cornmeal will do here, including yellow, white, blue, or red. Be adventurous!

Soft Flatbread from Across the Narrow Sea

In the Seven Kingdoms, nearly everyone enjoys loaves of hearty bread with their meals. But across the narrow sea, Daenerys, Tyrion, and many others prefer plates of soft flatbread to go with their figs, olives, and cheese. Even the Dornish royalty have adopted it to serve alongside their finest small plates. This variety—a simple pita bread—pairs nicely with Balerion Fish Roe Dip, Doran's Favorite Chickpea Paste (both in Chapter 2), cheese plates, and other exotic spreads and samplers. (*A Dance with Dragons*, Chapter 2—Daenerys)

MAKES 5 BREADS

1½ cups warm water
1 tablespoon honey
3½ teaspoons active dry
   yeast (2 packages)
1 tablespoon olive oil
1 tablespoon kosher salt
3–4 cups bread flour

1. In a medium bowl, stir together warm water, honey, and yeast, and set aside until foamy, about 10 minutes.
2. Stir in oil, salt, and enough bread flour to create a firm dough. Turn the dough out onto a floured surface and knead, adding flour only as necessary, until the dough becomes smooth and elastic, about 8–10 minutes. Return to bowl, cover with plastic wrap, and set in a warm place to rise until doubled in volume, about 1½ hours.
3. Preheat oven to 500°F, and preheat a dry baking sheet. Turn dough onto a floured surface, divide into 5 equal portions, and roll each into a tight ball. Using a rolling pin, roll out each ball into a flat disk, ¼-inch thick. Rest 20 minutes, uncovered.
4. Place one disk onto the preheated baking sheet. Bake exactly 3 minutes. Remove carefully with tongs, and repeat with remaining disks. Finished bread will be puffed and very pale. Cool completely before slicing and opening.

A Word of Wisdom

Don't brown your flatbread! This bread must remain pale if it is to be flexible. If you let it get too dark, it will become hard like a cracker. Watch the clock carefully unless you prefer your flatbreads to be quite crispy!

TRIDENT FLAX AND FENNEL HARDBREAD

Brienne and Jaime may be an odd pair of companions, but they at least agree that starving in the Riverlands is not an option conducive to long life. Hardbread may not be the most appealing meal for a Lannister who prefers the finer, softer luxuries in life, but it keeps them well on their march. This version spruces up the traditional flour-and-water combination and adds a provincial, earthy taste with a little grain and herb. (*A Storm of Swords,* Chapter 11—Jaime)

MAKES 12–15 CRACKERS

⅔ cup warm water
⅓ cup olive oil
½ teaspoon salt
1 teaspoon baking powder
1 tablespoon flax seeds
1 tablespoon fennel seeds
2–3 cups whole wheat
  flour
1 egg white

1. In a large bowl combine water, oil, and salt. Add baking powder, flax and fennel seeds, and enough flour to create a firm dough. Turn out onto a floured surface and knead, adding flour only to reduce stickiness, for 5 minutes. Return to bowl, dust with flour, cover with plastic wrap, and rest at room temperature for 15 minutes. Preheat oven to 400°F.

2. Coat a baking sheet with pan spray. Turn dough out onto a floured surface and divide it into 3 equal portions. Using a rolling pin, roll each portion to ¼-inch thick, and pierce each piece all over with a fork. Brush with egg white, arrange on baking sheet, and bake until edges are brown, about 10–15 minutes. When cool, break crackers into serving-size pieces.

A WORD OF WISDOM

Hardbread, also known as hardtack, could chip sailors' teeth after a while. Better to make a cracker version like this one than trouble yourself with a long-lasting loaf.

CHAPTER 4

FIRESIDE FARE:
Soups, Stews, and Salads

I n a realm where winters last for years and bring with them a unimaginable, bone-chilling cold, warm soups and stews become an essential meal. Fit for all tastes, ingredients, and occasions, these hearth-fired and cauldron-cooked dishes can accommodate anyone's means and needs.

A good salad is key as well. Whether the ingredients are cultivated or foraged, these vegetable dishes may be lighter fare, but are still a staple of a well-rounded diet. Reminiscent of the summer's "salad days," they may be the last holdouts of warmer times, too. Because they're susceptible to the coming deep freeze, large bowls of greenery will become more and more scarce as food stores dwindle in winter, but the wealthy and noble may enjoy their greens for a little while longer.

When vitality and health are so prized, cherished, and important to survival in a harsh world, soups, stews, and salads not only help the people of Westeros to make it through the harsher times, but remind them that nature moves in cycles and warmer times will come again.

Redwyne Brown Stock

The noble house of Highgarden—and possibly the entire world—counts House Redwyne as an indispensable asset in war and winemaking. Though sour Dornish wines and sweet Myrish varietals get plenty of praise, there's nothing as comforting, elegant, and delectable to a Westrosian as an unmistakable Arbor red from Redwyne's vineyards. As practical as its inspiration is prized, this stock can form the base for soups, stews, and roasts in just about any kitchen. (*A Game of Thrones*, Chapter 29—Sansa)

MAKES 1 GALLON

1 tablespoon olive oil

5 pounds bone-in meat of your choice

3 large yellow onions, peeled and roughly chopped

½ pound carrots, peeled and roughly chopped

3 stalks celery, peeled and roughly chopped

1 cup chopped tomatoes (fresh or canned), roughly chopped

1 bunch fresh parsley stems and leaves, chopped and separated

3 gallons water

1 cup dry Arbor red wine

4 stems fresh thyme

2 dried bay leaves

10–20 peppercorns

Redwyne Brown Stock

(CONTINUED)

1. Preheat oven to 400°F.
2. Place the oil, meat, and all the vegetables in a large roasting pan; brown in the oven for approximately 45 minutes, stirring frequently to prevent burning. Then, transfer all the meat and vegetables to a large stockpot with the water.
3. Place the roasting pan on the stovetop on medium heat; pour in the wine to deglaze the pan, gently stirring all the residue from the bottom of the pan. Pour this mixture into the stockpot with the meat and vegetables.
4. Simmer, uncovered, for 8 to 12 hours. Add the herbs and peppercorns; continue to simmer for 30 minutes. Remove from heat, strain, and place pan of strained stock in ice water to cool. Remove all fat that solidifies on the surface.

A Word of Wisdom

You can make this stock for any recipe you wish; just substitute in your preferred meat so the flavor will match your dish of choice. Beef and auroch might be the most versatile additions.

THE HAND'S DAUGHTER'S PUMPKIN SOUP

This thick, sweet soup satisfies Arya's stomach, but it doesn't fill her father's seat in the very large Small Hall of King's Landing. This dish easily recalls family dinners and intimate celebrations, possibly highlighting Ned's absence rather than easing it. (*A Game of Thrones*, Chapter 22—Arya)

SERVES 4

3 cups pulp from baked pie pumpkins
1 cup chicken or vegetable stock
1 cup heavy cream
1 green onion, chopped
⅓ cup fresh parsley
Dash ground ginger
Salt and pepper to taste
Crème fraîche or sour cream for garnish

1. Combine pumpkin pulp, stock, heavy cream, green onion, and parsley in a blender container. Pulse to combine; process until puréed.
2. Pour in a saucepan; cook over medium heat until hot. Stir in ginger, salt, and pepper to taste. Serve with a dollop of crème fraîche or sour cream for garnish.

A WORD OF WISDOM
It is better to use small pie pumpkins for cooking rather than the larger ones, which are more suited to being carved into jack-o-lanterns.

Harrenhal Vegetable Stew

Stews don't always need meat to be delicious—but empty revenge is never satisfying. Weasel enjoys her barley stew well enough, but the score she decides to have settled is a bit thin. Still, this healthy meal of vegetables helps her mind renew its vigor for the dark work that lies ahead. (*A Clash of Kings*, Chapter 30—Arya)

<u>**SERVES 6**</u>

1 onion, chopped
2 carrots, sliced
2 ribs celery, chopped
2 tablespoons olive oil
8 cups vegetable broth
1 cup barley, uncooked
1½ cups frozen mixed
   vegetables
1 14-ounce can crushed or
   diced tomatoes
½ teaspoon parsley
½ teaspoon thyme
2 bay leaves
Salt and pepper to taste

1. In a large soup or stockpot, sauté the onion, carrots, and celery in olive oil for 3–5 minutes, just until onions are almost soft.
2. Reduce heat to medium low, and add remaining ingredients, except salt and pepper.
3. Bring to a simmer, cover, and allow to cook for at least 45 minutes, stirring occasionally.
4. Remove cover and allow to cook for 10 more minutes.
5. Remove bay leaves; season with salt and pepper to taste.

A Word of Wisdom

Stews can be as creative as you like, but remember these tips to make them perfect: Before you add liquid, sear meat (if using) to add caramelized flavor and rich color to the stew. Cut all vegetables into similar-size pieces so they cook evenly. Always add the starches last!

HAND OF THE KING'S OXTAIL SOUP

This old and fine meal turns an easily overlooked part of the animal into a tender, rich meal fit for the King's Hand. Equally methodical as a chef—though often with less time to cook up his last-minute schemes—Tyrion sups on this soup, prepared for him by the finest chef to be found in King's Landing. Cooked for hours, the oxtails will be tender and choice by the time the soup is ready to serve. (*A Clash of Kings,* Chapter 8—Tyrion)

SERVES 6

2 pounds oxtails

1 medium onion, diced

2 carrots, diced

2 leeks, sliced

1 celery rib, diced

3 garlic cloves, minced

8 ounces mushrooms, sliced

1 large russet potato, peeled and diced

8 cups Redwyne Brown Stock (in this chapter), made with beef, auroch, or ox

2 bay leaves

¼ cup red wine

¼ cup minced fresh parsley

Salt and pepper to taste

HAND OF THE KING'S OXTAIL SOUP
(CONTINUED)

1. Place oxtails in a single layer on a roasting pan; roast in 400°F oven 40 minutes, turning occasionally.
2. Remove oxtails from oven; place on a platter. Drain fat from roasting pan; set aside. Pour 1 cup of water in pan; stir to deglaze.
3. In a heavy soup pot, combine 2 tablespoons of fat from roasted oxtails, onion, carrots, leeks, celery, garlic, and mushrooms. Sauté 5 minutes over high heat.
4. Add potato, broth, and water from roasting pan; bring to a boil.
5. Add bay leaves and wine; reduce heat to medium. Add oxtails; simmer 2 hours.
6. Add parsley, salt, and pepper; remove from heat. Let stand a few minutes before serving.

A WORD OF WISDOM
You may need to order oxtail from your butcher ahead of time. If you find yourself fresh out of oxtail, you can substitute necks, shanks, ribs, or other soup bones from veal, beef, or auroch.

RANGING SOUP OF ROOTS

Protecting the realms of men is hungry work. Meats can be cumbersome to carry during journeys where stealth is essential. A soup of hearty roots cooked over a campfire feeds the ranging Night's Watch efficiently, vegetarian or no. Add foraged roots or garden-grown root vegetables to capture the wild, hearty spirit of this soup. (*A Clash of Kings*, Chapter 43—Jon)

SERVES 8–10

1 quart water

2 cups stinging nettle greens, chopped

4–6 evening primrose roots, peeled and chopped

4–6 Jerusalem artichoke tubers, chopped

1 cup chopped roots, combination of dandelion roots, burdock roots,
yellow dock roots, or other roots, depending on what's available

½ cup rock tripe broken up into small pieces

2 tablespoons vegetable oil or butter

1 medium onion, chopped

2 celery stalks, chopped

3 carrots, chopped

Field garlic or wild onion tops, chopped

1 dried cayenne or chili pepper

½ teaspoon evening primrose seeds

Salt and pepper to taste

RANGING SOUP OF ROOTS

(CONTINUED)

1. Heat water to boiling in a medium-size soup pot.
2. Add nettles and let cook for 2 minutes.
3. Add evening primrose roots, Jerusalem artichokes, chopped roots, and rock tripe.
4. Heat oil or butter in saucepan and sauté onions, celery, and carrots.
5. Add to soup pot, along with field garlic or onion tops, pepper, and evening primrose seeds. Cook on medium-low heat for at least 30 minutes. Season with salt and pepper to taste.

A WORD OF WISDOM

Leave the roots a bit chunky in this soup for the best variety of textures. Just make sure that you chop the foraged roots into pieces that will cook to your liking in 30 minutes. Of course, you'll need to learn to identify what is safe to forage and what isn't before you head out to gather. In a pinch, you can substitute root vegetables like turnips and parsnips for the foraged roots.

CERSEI'S CREAMY CHESTNUT SOUP

Tyrion may suspect Cersei's motives, but he does not question his sister's taste in food. Chestnuts seem to be a foil to the Queen: while the raw, spiny fruit looks ominous to the passerby, Cersei's menace is less apparent, except to those who know her as well as Tyrion does and, like him, are clever enough to survive obtaining such insight. But once chestnuts are roasted, boiled, and puréed—all of which Cersei might do to those who threaten her person or power—they can be all sweetness and delight. (*A Clash of Kings*, Chapter 44—Tyrion)

SERVES 8

2 pounds chestnuts, roasted

1 tablespoon butter or chicken fat

6 leeks, well-trimmed and thinly sliced

1 carrot, thinly sliced

1 rib celery, thinly sliced

Pinch thyme

8 cups chicken broth

¼ cup minced fresh parsley

Salt and pepper to taste

CERSEI'S CREAMY CHESTNUT SOUP
(CONTINUED)

1. Preheat oven to 400°F. Cut an X into each chestnut on the flat side.
2. Place on a baking sheet and bake for 30–35 minutes, turning frequently. Peel while still warm. Chop chestnuts coarsely and set aside.
3. In a soup pot, melt butter or fat over medium-high heat. Add leeks; sauté 3 minutes. Add carrot and celery; continue to sauté 2 minutes longer.
4. Add chestnuts and thyme, and cook for 1 minute.
5. Add broth to pot; bring mixture to a boil. Reduce heat to medium; simmer 30 minutes or until chestnuts are very tender. Remove from heat and let cool briefly.
6. Blend in batches to purée soup. Strain through a fine sieve into a fresh pot. Reheat soup, then season with parsley, salt, and pepper.

A WORD OF WISDOM

This recipe is a play on cock-a-leekie soup, which doesn't traditionally feature chestnuts. Cock-a-leekie is usually garnished with thinly sliced prunes to add nutritional value.

QUEEN'S WHITE BEAN SOUP

Queen Cersei's food may be decadent, but she often has ulterior motives when she sits down to share her meal. With a battle on her doorstep, Cersei's dinner with her brother is especially tempting—so much so that Tyrion thinks twice before eating anything she doesn't. This fragrant soup, inspired by Cersei's dish of white beans and bacon, would loosen anyone's lips as trouble brews. (*A Clash of Kings*, Chapter 44—Tyrion)

<u>SERVES 10</u>

2 pounds hot Italian sausage

3 yellow onions

4 sprigs thyme

4 tablespoons virgin olive oil

2 gallons Redwyne Brown Stock (this chapter), made with beef

2 pounds cooked cannellini beans

1 large bulb garlic

1 cup black olives, pitted

¼ bunch fresh parsley, cleaned and chopped

Kosher salt

Freshly cracked black pepper

1 loaf fresh Italian bread, thinly sliced

About ⅔ cup store-bought roasted red pepper purée

QUEEN'S WHITE BEAN SOUP
(CONTINUED)

1. Cut the sausage into slices about ½ inch thick. Peel and finely slice the onions. Clean the thyme and remove the leaves (discard the stems).

2. Heat 1 tablespoon of the virgin oil over medium temperature in a large stockpot. Brown the sausage for 3 minutes. Add the onions and cook for 1 minute (do not brown the onions).

3. Add the stock and simmer on low heat for 1 hour, uncovered. Add the beans and simmer for 30 minutes, uncovered.

4. After adding the beans, prepare a garlic paste. Preheat oven to 400°F. Slice the unpeeled bulb in half crosswise. Place halves face-down on a sheet of foil large enough to cover both. Form sheet into a packet around garlic without fully covering. Pour 1 tablespoon of the oil into foil packet, ensuring cut faces of bulb are covered in oil. Wrap garlic completely; make sure all edges are folded up to prevent oil from leaking out. Place packet in oven.

5. Roast for 10 minutes, until the garlic is completely softened.

6. Let cool, and then peel. Mash half of the garlic for garnish and set aside.

7. Purée remaining half of garlic with olives in a food processor. Add the parsley, salt, pepper, and remaining 2 tablespoons oil, and blend thoroughly.

8. Lay slices of bread on a baking sheet and bake in oven on 400°F for 10 minutes. Spread garlic and olive purée on bread.

9. Ladle the soup into bowls. Garnish each serving with about 1 tablespoon of the red pepper purée, ½ teaspoon of the reserved garlic paste, and a few thyme leaves.

A WORD OF WISDOM

For easier-to-cut raw sausages, freeze them for about 30 minutes before you slice them. Just let them thaw a little before cooking.

LATE LORD FREY'S LEEK SOUP

Pale and cold, this is the perfect dish for the ancient and devious Lord Walder Frey of the Crossing. It's also an appropriate and delectable allusion to the heartless destruction of those he deems his enemies, and far more palatable than the stewed crow and maggots Robb Stark swore he'd eat to please the Freys. For a touch of irony, serve it with bread and salt—just don't serve it at a wedding. (*A Storm of Swords*, Chapter 51—Catelyn)

SERVES 6

4 tablespoons (½ stick) butter
4 leeks, white and light green parts, sliced
1 medium onion, diced
3 pounds russet potatoes, peeled and thinly sliced
5 cups chicken broth
Salt and pepper to taste
1 cup heavy cream
Chopped fresh parsley or chives

1. In a large soup pot, melt butter over medium-high heat. Add leeks and onion; cook, stirring often, just until vegetables soften—do not brown. Add potatoes and broth; bring to a boil. Reduce heat to medium; simmer 1 hour, or until potatoes are very soft.
2. Remove from heat. Either purée soup in a food processor or press through a fine mesh strainer into a bowl. Season with salt and pepper.
3. Chill until ready to serve. Before serving, whisk in heavy cream. Check seasoning. Ladle into bowls; garnish with parsley or chives.

A WORD OF WISDOM

If you prefer your leek soup warm, by all means, enjoy. Just return it to the saucepan after puréeing, add cream, and heat—do not boil. No need to curdle this traitor's soup, too!

LORD NESTOR ROYCE'S WILD MUSHROOM RAGOUT

To get their caravan moving down the Giant's Lance, Alayne promises little Lord Robert Arryn mushroom soup and venison and lemon cakes at Lord Nestor Royce's feast—but it may be Alayne who needs real fortification after the harrowing journey. Sturdy and satisfying, this Royce-inspired ragout would welcome any traveler off a cold, dangerous path.
(*A Feast for Crows*, Chapter 41—Alayne)

SERVES 4–6

1 pound wild mushrooms
   (morels, shiitake, cremini,
   or oyster)
¼ cup (½ stick) butter
1 leek, cleaned and tender
   white part sliced
2 cloves garlic, minced
¼ cup dry white wine
½ cup heavy cream
Kosher salt and freshly
   ground white or black
   pepper to taste

1. Brush mushrooms clean and remove any tough stems. Slice larger mushrooms, halve medium-size, and leave small ones whole. Set aside.
2. Melt butter in a large skillet over medium-high heat. Add sliced leek and sauté for a minute. Add garlic and cook for another minute. Then add mushrooms. Toss to coat and cook until tender and browned, about 3 to 4 minutes. Add wine and cook until reduced by half. Add cream and bring just to a boil. Season to taste with salt and pepper and serve hot.

A WORD OF WISDOM

Sometimes it is best to buy exotic or wild mushrooms dried. Reconstitute them in warm water for about an hour, until flexible. Discard the water.

VOLANTENE COLD BEET SOUP

"Sweet" is a word Quentyn Martell uses to describe Volantis and he means it both accurately and ironically. In his time there, he finds people most unhelpful in the hot, humid city that is known for its Triarch rulers constantly scheming against each other, as those who belong to the Tigers or the Elephants will do what they must to influence votes and politics. And yet, they do love their sweet wines and sweet beets. An accurate picture of Volantene tastes, this soup is a strangely skewed reflection of many of its people. (*A Dance with Dragons*, Chapter 6— The Merchant's Man)

SERVES 6–8

4 cups fresh beets, peeled
and shredded
1 whole onion, peeled and
stuck with 4 cloves
2 quarts water
¼ cup lemon juice
2 tablespoons sugar
3 eggs
Salt and pepper to taste
Sour cream

1. In a soup pot, combine beets, onion, and water; bring to a boil over high heat. Reduce heat to medium; simmer 1 hour, or until shredded beets are tender.
2. Remove onion and cloves; discard. Stir in lemon juice and sugar; continue cooking 30 minutes.
3. Place eggs in food processor; pulse to whip. Ladle 2 cups soup into large, heat-safe measuring cup. With processor running, slowly pour soup into eggs. Immediately stir egg mixture back into soup pot; stir well. Add salt and pepper to taste.
4. Allow soup to cool; refrigerate until chilled. Serve cold with a dollop of sour cream on top.

A WORD OF WISDOM

Remove the skins of cooked beets with less mess by simply wrapping them in a clean, dry kitchen towel and rubbing the thin outer skin right off while they are still warm. Fair warning: beets will color your towel red, but most of it will wash out.

NIGHT'S WATCH ONION SOUP

Though its flavor is common, this soup is filling and flavorful enough to pass for wedding fare at the Wall. Jon Snow mourns the dwindling supply of butter, but he might be surprised to know that this soup could be a victim to winter's toll on their stores as well. With little green food left to feed milk cows, butter would be an early casualty of the long winter. Some substitutions might be made with salt and lard or oil, but it would be hard to replicate this soup's simple creaminess. (*A Dance with Dragons*, Chapter 49—Jon)

SERVES 8

6 yellow onions, thinly
  sliced
6 tablespoons butter
4 cups Redwyne Brown
  Stock (in this chapter),
  made with goat
½ teaspoon salt
½ teaspoon black
  peppercorns
¼ pound fresh Parmesan
  cheese, grated
1 medium carrot, shredded

1. Slowly sauté onions in butter in pan over low heat until browned.
2. Add onions, broth, salt, and peppercorns to a slow cooker.
3. Cover and heat on a low setting for 3 to 4 hours.
4. Before serving, stir ¼ cup grated cheese into the soup. Set out the remainder of the cheese and shredded carrot to garnish individual servings.

A WORD OF WISDOM

Dress this or any soup or salad with homemade croutons. Simply cube your bread of choice and place on a baking sheet. Sprinkle the bread with Parmesan cheese and freshly ground black pepper, then broil until the bread is browned. Winterfell Black Bread or Black Brothers' Oat Bread (both in Chapter 3) would be familiar enough to the Night's Watch to fit with this soup.

COMMON PEASE PORRIDGE

At times, Tyrion rather enjoys just how much people underestimate him due to his stature and appearance. He can seem as unassuming as a dish of Common Pease Porridge, when he's actually moving his pawns through the game of life, cornering enemies and their agents with a smile. Like Tyrion, this pease porridge shouldn't be taken lightly: this classic variation of pea soup can come quite close to beating back the push of cold, Northern winds . . . at least for a while. (*A Clash of Kings*, Chapter 17—Theon)

SERVES 6

6 strips bacon, diced

2 stalks celery, finely diced

3 large carrots, peeled

1 large sweet onion, peeled and diced

2 cups dried split peas, soaked overnight, drained and rinsed

2 cups chicken broth

3 cups water

2 large potatoes, peeled and diced

1 smoked ham hock

4 ounces smoked sausage or ham, diced

Salt and freshly ground black pepper to taste

COMMON PEASE PORRIDGE
(CONTINUED)

1. Add the bacon and celery to the slow cooker; cover and cook on high while you prepare the carrots. Grate half of one of the carrots and dice the remaining carrots. Add the grated carrot and diced onion to the slow cooker; stir to mix them in with the bacon and celery. Cover and cook on high for 30 minutes or until the onions are transparent.

2. Add the diced carrots, split peas, broth, water, potatoes, ham hock, and smoked sausage or ham to the slow cooker. Cover and cook on low for 8 hours or until the peas are soft.

3. Use a slotted spoon to remove the ham hock; remove the meat from the bone and set aside. Mash peas until smooth then return ham to porridge. Alternately, add ham directly into porridge and purée until smooth with an immersion blender. Taste for seasoning and add salt and pepper if needed.

A WORD OF WISDOM

Because the sodium content in the broth and meats can affect the flavor, wait until the soup is cooked and, when you taste it for seasoning, add salt if needed.

LORD CASWELL'S VENISON AND BARLEY STEW

In Westeros, political intrigue deepens at the drop of a pin and violent conflict flies as fast as any salacious gossip. But inside the dining hall of Lord Caswell of Bitterbridge, there is a semblance of peace and security—even if it is a carefully cultivated one. This venison stew would distract any traveling guests from the reality of battle, reminding them of times of plenty spent with their family and friends. Ward off animosity with hearty portions and comfortable conversation. (*A Clash of Kings*, Chapter 22—Catelyn)

SERVES 6–8

3 pounds venison stew
  meat
4 tablespoons olive oil
5 cups beef bouillon
1 cup beer
2 envelopes peppercorn
  gravy mix
2 teaspoons oregano
1 bay leaf
2 cloves garlic, minced
2 cups pearl onions
½ cup pearl barley
4 potatoes
6 carrots

1. Brown venison in oil in a large Dutch oven. Combine beef bouillon, beer, gravy mix, oregano, bay leaf, garlic, onions, and barley.
2. Bring to a boil, cover, and reduce heat to a simmer for 1 hour.
3. Peel and cut potatoes and carrots. Add to stew and simmer for about 30 minutes or until vegetables are fork tender.
4. Remove bay leaf. Serve in bowls.

A WORD OF WISDOM

There may be no better side dish for this than a just-baked loaf of Inn at the Crossroads 7-Grain Loaf (Chapter 3).

Inn of the Kneeling Man's Rabbit Stew

Rain, gray skies, long journeys, and strange companions matter little when Sharna the inn-keep is willing to stew rabbits in ale and onions for her diners. Such filling roadside fare would seduce many a traveler as hungry as Hot Pie into a sense of false security. But Squab isn't so easily distracted; she feasts away but stays wary. (*A Storm of Swords*, Chapter 13—Arya)

SERVES 4–6

3 slices bacon

1 (2- to 3-pound) rabbit, cut into pieces

1 cup seasoned flour

3–4 tablespoons vegetable oil or bacon grease

1 onion, sliced

1 clove garlic, minced

4 sprigs Italian parsley, chopped

1 (8-ounce) can chopped tomatoes, preferably Italian Roma

1 teaspoon dried basil

1 teaspoon dried oregano

¼ cup ale

Kosher salt and freshly ground pepper to taste

1. Fry bacon in a large skillet until crisp and set aside. Dredge pieces of rabbit meat in seasoned flour. Sauté in 3 to 4 tablespoons oil or bacon grease over medium-high heat until well browned. Place all meat in a slow cooker.

2. Sauté onion and garlic in same skillet for about 4 to 5 minutes over medium heat. Spoon into slow cooker. Add the parsley, tomatoes and juice, herbs, and ale and season to taste. Cook over low heat for 6 to 8 hours. Serve hot.

A Word of Wisdom

Rabbit meat has the texture of stewing chicken, with a slightly sweeter, gamier flavor. If you aren't fond of rabbit, you can always substitute chicken or duck.

KING STANNIS'S FISH STEW

In the Great Hall set in the mouth of a stone dragon, new alliances are forged and symbols of the old order are destroyed. What better dish for King Stannis Baratheon's table than a red fish stew? With just a hint of fire, this meal honors R'hllor, his Red Priestess Melisandre of Asshai, and the bloody path Stannis wants to cut to the Iron Throne. (*A Clash of Kings*—Prologue)

SERVES 4

2 tablespoons olive oil

1 tablespoon butter

1 onion, finely diced

1 small bell pepper, cored and diced

2 garlic cloves, minced

1 jalapeño pepper, minced

1 (28-ounce) can tomatoes

1 (8-ounce) can tomato sauce

1 cup red wine

1 tablespoon red wine vinegar

3 cups shellfish or fish broth

2 bay leaves

1 teaspoon fresh oregano leaves

1 sprig fresh rosemary

Salt to taste

12 large shrimp, peeled

12 small clams, scrubbed

12 mussels, scrubbed

8 cracked stone crab claws or 4 cleaned blue crab halves

⅓ cup minced parsley

Freshly ground black pepper to taste

KING STANNIS'S FISH STEW
(CONTINUED)

1. In a large, heavy soup pot or Dutch oven, combine olive oil and butter. Over medium-high heat, sauté onion, bell pepper, garlic, and jalapeño pepper until vegetables are crisp-tender, about 3 minutes.
2. Add tomatoes, tomato sauce, wine, vinegar, broth, bay leaves, oregano, and rosemary. Bring to a boil; reduce heat and simmer 20 minutes.
3. Remove bay leaves and rosemary sprig; add salt, shrimp, clams, mussels, and crab. Cover and simmer just until clams and mussels open and shrimp turn opaque, about 2 to 3 minutes.
4. Add parsley and pepper. Divide shrimp and other shellfish among 4 bowls; ladle broth over the seafood. Serve with hot, crusty bread from Chapter 3.

A Word of Wisdom

If you prefer not to pick shells from your food, just steam the clams, mussels, and crab in a separate pot, strain the resulting broth into the stew, and add the shelled clams, mussels, and crab to the stew at the last minute.

Northern Harvest Auroch Stew

A good cut of auroch makes for a substantial stew fit for feasting warriors and nobility. Though he is seen as weak by some of those around him at the harvest festival, Bran Stark knows he has strength within, and though he chooses a beef-and-barley stew in front of his guests, trading up for auroch might have done even more to keep that strength up. This recipe works well for both. (*A Clash of Kings*, Chapter 16—Bran)

<u>**SERVES 8**</u>

⅓ cup vegetable oil

2 pounds boneless auroch or beef chuck roast, cut in large pieces

2 pound flank steak, cut in pieces

2 large onions, sliced

2 cloves garlic, minced

1 cup dry kidney beans

1 cup dry lima beans

6 cups beef broth

⅓ cup ketchup

1 cup dry pearl barley

6 white potatoes, peeled and cut in large chunks

Salt and pepper to taste

Northern Harvest Auroch Stew

(CONTINUED)

1. Heat vegetable oil in a Dutch oven. Brown beef pieces; set aside. Add onions; sauté until onion softens, about 3 minutes.
2. Add garlic and beans; sauté 3–5 minutes.
3. Stir in broth, ketchup, and barley. Return beef to pot; stir. Add potatoes, salt, and pepper; adjust liquid to make sure beef is covered. Bring to a boil; remove from heat. Cover Dutch oven tightly.
4. Place Dutch oven in 200°F oven 10–15 hours. Check occasionally to make sure broth hasn't been absorbed or evaporated. Serve in bowls.

A Word of Wisdom

Gage served this stew with loaves of Winterfell Black Bread (Chapter 3) and a side of Winterfell Cold Fruit Soup (Chapter 2). A generous helping of The Dead Man's Roasted Vegetables (Chapter 3) and Ballroom Blackberry Honeycake (Chapter 6) would finish this meal off nobly.

LEAF'S BLOOD STEW

Bran receives quite an education north of the Wall. As he fills his mind with seeing and reading and the secrets of the weirwoods, he fills his belly with Blood Stew made by Leaf and her fellow singers. Any wild game will do to make this an interesting meal for those natural travelers with a taste for wide horizons. (*A Dance with Dragons*, Chapter 34—Bran)

SERVES 8

2–3 pounds rabbit, squirrel, or other small game

2 tablespoons oil

Kosher salt and freshly ground black pepper to taste

1 pound spicy sausage (Italian, andouille, or game)

4 tablespoons (½ stick) unsalted butter

2 onions, chopped

1 green bell pepper, chopped

3–4 stalks celery, chopped

8 ounces fresh mushrooms, sliced

2 cloves garlic, minced

6 tablespoons all-purpose flour

8 cups chicken broth, divided

1 cup game blood, chilled with any solids well-mashed

1 cup fire-roasted red pepper, chopped

½ teaspoon red pepper flakes

1 teaspoon dried thyme

2 bay leaves

LEAF'S BLOOD STEW

(CONTINUED)

1. Preheat the oven to 400°F. Cut small game into pieces. Rub the meat with 2 tablespoons oil and season with salt and pepper. Place in a roasting pan and cook for about 45 to 60 minutes, or until tender. Remove and let cool. Pick meat off the bones and set aside.

2. Brown sausage in a large pot or Dutch oven over medium-high heat. Add butter, onions, pepper, celery, mushrooms, and garlic. Sauté for about 10 to 12 minutes, stirring slowly. Stir in flour to form a roux (paste) and cook for about 3 or 4 minutes. Slowly add 2 cups of the chicken broth and 1 cup blood, stirring to combine; then add the rest of the broth, red peppers, red pepper flakes, thyme, bay leaves, and game meat.

3. Bring the mixture to a gentle boil, lower the heat, and simmer, uncovered, for 2 hours. If mixture is too thick, add 1 or 2 cups of water or additional chicken broth. Season to taste with salt and pepper. Remove bay leaves before serving.

A WORD OF WISDOM

Blood may sound like an exotic, intimidating ingredient, but it is a common ingredient in cultures that value every part of an animal. Add a dash of vinegar to keep it from congealing when you store it.

THREE-FINGER HOBB'S BEST MUTTON

Three-Finger Hobb won't see a brother of the black go hungry. With Hobb in the kitchen and Owen the Oaf as server, it's a sure thing that food is brought to all those who serve on the Wall, rain or shine. A pailful of this fine stew with its spices, onions, and ale is an excellent way to end a day's work or to begin a long night's watch. (*A Storm of Swords*, Chapter 55—Jon)

<u>SERVES 6–8</u>

6 strips bacon

3 pounds boneless mutton shoulder

⅓ cup flour

1 teaspoon kosher salt

1 teaspoon black pepper

½ teaspoon garlic powder

¼ teaspoon paprika

2 medium onions, diced

2 cloves garlic, minced

4 cups beef or mutton broth

1 teaspoon sugar

1 cup stout ale

2 bay leaves

½ teaspoon thyme leaves

1 large leek, trimmed and sliced

3 pounds white potatoes, peeled and cut into chunks

3 cups thickly sliced carrots

1½ cups green peas, frozen or shelled fresh

Salt and pepper to taste

⅓ cup minced fresh parsley

THREE-FINGER HOBB'S BEST MUTTON
(CONTINUED)

1. In a large, heavy frying pan, cook bacon until crisp; set aside, leaving the bacon fat in the pan. Trim fat from mutton; cut into 1½-inch cubes. Combine flour, salt, pepper, garlic powder, and paprika. Dredge mutton pieces in the flour mixture; shake off excess flour. Brown meat in the bacon fat over medium-high heat; remove to Dutch oven.

2. Sauté onions in the same skillet over medium-high heat until browned. Add garlic; stir well. Pour 1 cup of broth in skillet; stir to scrape browned bits from bottom of pan. Pour broth, onions, and garlic over mutton in Dutch oven. Add remaining broth, sugar, ale, bay leaves, thyme, and bacon.

3. Place Dutch oven over high heat; bring to a boil. Reduce heat to medium; cook, stirring occasionally, 1½ hours. Add additional stock or water if needed.

4. Remove bay leaves from Dutch oven. Add leek, potatoes, carrots, and peas; cover and cook until potatoes are tender, about 20–30 minutes.

5. Remove from heat; add salt, pepper, and parsley. Serve in shallow bowls.

A WORD OF WISDOM

What lamb is available and where it comes from may vary wildly by season. True lamb aficionados often prefer lamb from one region over another, citing flavor and texture differences.

SWEETROBIN'S STEWED GOAT

High above the Vale, surrounded by ice and rock and open air, Lord Robert Arryn and his companions pick their way down the treacherous Giant's Lance, but trials of a journey are nothing when a hot meal of stewed goat awaits. The sure-footed caprines would be a steady source of fiber, milk, and meat for peasant and peer in the lands protected by the Mountains of the Moon. (*A Feast for Crows*, Chapter 41—Alayne)

SERVES 6–8

2½ pounds goat meat

1 teaspoon kosher salt

1 teaspoon black pepper

1 teaspoon cayenne pepper

½ teaspoon garlic powder

¼ teaspoon paprika

⅓ cup flour

5 tablespoons olive oil

1 medium onion, diced

4 cups beef broth

2 cloves garlic, minced

1 rib celery, sliced

6 ounces mushrooms, sliced

1 teaspoon Worcestershire sauce

1 cup dry red wine

3 pounds red potatoes, peeled and quartered

2 cups baby carrots

Salt and pepper to taste

¼ cup minced fresh parsley

SWEETROBIN'S STEWED GOAT

(CONTINUED)

1. Trim fat from goat; cut into 1½-inch cubes. Combine salt, black and cayenne peppers, garlic powder, and paprika; stir well. Liberally sprinkle seasoning mixture over goat; toss. (You may not use all of the spice mix. Reserve leftover mix for later use.) Sprinkle a small amount of flour over goat, just enough to coat cubes lightly.

2. In a heavy Dutch oven over medium-high heat, brown goat in oil. Working in batches, remove browned cubes to bowl using slotted spoon. Add half of onion to oil; sauté 3 minutes.

3. Sprinkle oil and onion with remaining flour; stir until flour begins to brown. Whisk in 1 cup of the broth; continue stirring until browned bits have been pulled from bottom and sauce is smooth. Add remaining onion, garlic, celery, and mushrooms; return goat to pot. Reduce heat to medium; simmer 2 minutes.

4. Add remaining broth, Worcestershire sauce, and wine; simmer uncovered 2 hours, stirring occasionally.

5. Add potatoes and carrots; cook until potatoes are tender, about 20–30 minutes.

6. Remove from heat. Add salt, pepper, and parsley.

A WORD OF WISDOM

If goat isn't to your liking, you can quite easily turn this into a beef stew. Just substitute a brisket or bottom round roast for goat meat.

SISTER'S STEW

Davos may not find much sweet about the island of Sweetsister, but the stew is uncharacteristically fine. Enjoyed throughout the Three Sisters by everyone from Lord Godric Borrell to the silent serving boy Wex, this stew combines artfully pirated spices and fresh seafood to give a flavor that invigorates the taste buds and warms travelers down to their bones. (*A Dance with Dragons*, Chapter 9—Davos)

SERVES 4

1 dozen small clams, scrubbed

2 cups white wine

2 cups clam juice

2 bay leaves

1 sprig thyme

¼ teaspoon crushed saffron threads

1 tablespoon butter

2 shallots, minced

2 garlic cloves

1 leek, chopped

2 cups half-and-half

1 pound crabmeat of at least three varieties (see A Word of Wisdom)

3 tablespoons crab roe

Salt and pepper to taste

2 tablespoons minced fresh parsley

2 tablespoons minced fresh chervil

2 cups barley, cooked

SISTER'S STEW

(CONTINUED)

1. Place cleaned clams in a heavy soup pot or Dutch oven; pour in wine and clam juice. Add bay leaves, thyme sprig, and saffron threads; bring to a boil and cover well. Cook 5 minutes; clams should be done and shells open. Discard any unopened clams.

2. With a slotted spoon, remove clams in shells to a bowl. Strain cooking liquid through a fine sieve into another bowl. Melt butter over medium-high heat in soup pot. Add shallots, garlic, and leeks; sauté 3 minutes.

3. Pour reserved cooking liquid from clams into pot. Bring to a boil; reduce heat to medium.

4. Reserve 8 clams in shells; remove meat from remaining clams. Coarsely chop meat; add to simmering liquid. Cook 5 minutes.

5. Add half-and-half; continue cooking 1 minute. Do not allow to boil. Stir in crabmeat and roe, cooking 1 additional minute.

6. Remove from heat; season with salt and pepper. Prepare 4 bowls with ½ cup cooked barley in each. Ladle soup into bowls; garnish with reserved clams in shells. Sprinkle parsley and chervil over each bowl. Serve immediately.

A WORD OF WISDOM

It takes 18–20 whole blue crabs to equal 1 pound of crabmeat, so it can get expensive. After the whole crabs are steamed and shelled, the meat is separated into three varieties: prized backfin lump crabmeat, white body crabmeat, and less expensive (but flavorful) claw crabmeat.

Lannister Cream Stews

A savory cream stew might charm many guests into relaxing, but not Tyrion Lannister. He can certainly appreciate such a dish, but he's liable to wonder (albeit briefly) what's behind such a rich, flavorful, changeable stew. Since any combination of fresh herbs—parsley, green onion, cilantro, basil, oregano, or tarragon—gives this soup new, pleasant flavor, it's entirely possible there's more to this meal than first meets the eye. (*A Clash of Kings*, Chapter 17—Tyrion)

SERVES 6

6 cups chicken broth
1 (15-ounce) can fire-
   roasted diced tomatoes
3 cups corn kernels
1 cup shredded cooked
   chicken
1 cup half-and-half
⅓ cup minced fresh herbs
Salt and pepper to taste

1. In a large saucepan, bring broth to a boil; add tomatoes and corn. Reduce heat to medium; simmer 10 minutes.
2. Stir in cooked chicken; continue cooking 5 minutes.
3. Add half-and-half and fresh herbs; cook just until heated through. Add salt and pepper to taste. Serve immediately.

A Word of Wisdom

Serve your soups and stews hot. Piping-hot foods will warm you up and encourage you to savor them more slowly.

Three-Finger Hobb's Infamous Three-Meat Stew

When the Night Watch's faithful cook can't serve up variety, he at least offers a nice dose of irony. Hobb's mutton-mutton-and-mutton combination goes down just as easily as any of his dishes, though, and it has a slightly lighter taste than his Best Mutton. (*A Dance with Dragons*, Chapter 21—Jon)

SERVES 4

2 leeks, white part only

2 mutton shoulder chops

¼ pound mutton shank, cubed

¼ pound mutton neck, cubed

⅓ cup pearl barley

1 large carrot, peeled and diced

1 stalk of celery, thinly sliced

2 medium potatoes, peeled and diced

6 cups water

Salt and freshly ground black pepper to taste

Fresh parsley, minced, optional

1. Dice the white part of the leeks; rinse well and drain. Add the leeks to a slow cooker along with the mutton, barley, carrot, celery, potatoes, water, salt, and pepper.
2. Cover and cook on low for 6 to 8 hours or until the meat is tender and the potatoes are cooked through.
3. Transfer half a mutton chop to each of four bowls and ladle juices and a helping of vegetables and cubed meat over top. Garnish with parsley if desired.

A Word of Wisdom

Lamb is technically meat of a sheep that is less than a year old, and mutton is meat from an older sheep. Mutton is tougher, fattier, and more intense in flavor, but is more popular in some cultures than others. If you prefer it, substitute lamb for mutton in any recipe in this book.

RIVERRUN TURNIP GREENS AND RED FENNEL SALAD

While songs and revelry fill the halls of the Tully family seat, Lady Catelyn and Brienne of Tarth have this ladylike salad with their supper. Brienne sees food as another chore, and this dignified dish probably didn't help alter that opinion. Even without the sweetgrass, this salad looks better for a soirée of demure noblewomen than a bold, would-be knight whom people only ironically call "beauty." Nevertheless, this recipe teems with personality—which Cat and Brienne both have in spades. (*A Clash of Kings*, Chapter 55—Catelyn)

SERVES 6

3 tablespoons lemon juice

4 teaspoons orange juice

½ teaspoon kosher salt

⅛ teaspoon cayenne pepper, ground

⅛ teaspoon black pepper, finely ground

3 tablespoons sesame oil

2 cups diced fresh apricots

⅓ cup sliced fennel bulb

¼ cup diced dried apricots

½ cup sliced celery

3 cups shredded turnip greens

1 cup alfalfa sprouts

¼ teaspoon orange zest

Riverrun Turnip Greens and Red Fennel Salad

(CONTINUED)

1. Whisk lemon juice, orange juice, salt, cayenne pepper, and black pepper together in a mixing bowl. Whisk until salt dissolves. Slowly pour oil into dressing and whisk until emulsified.
2. Add fresh apricots, fennel, dried apricots, and celery to the large bowl. Toss well to coat with dressing. Cover bowl and place in refrigerator. Let mixture marinate for 10 minutes.
3. Gently toss turnip greens and alfalfa sprouts together in a large salad bowl. Remove apricot mixture from fridge. Gently toss apricot mixture into salad, scraping the sides of the mixing bowl to make sure you get as much dressing as possible. Toss well to mix and coat. Garnish with a sprinkle of orange zest and serve.

A Word of Wisdom

Fennel salad can be prepared in advance and then left to marinate for an hour or so, giving the flavors time to develop.

BITTER GREEN SALAD

No one joins the Night's Watch purely out of a spirit of adventure or glory. Even those who believe it is a noble brotherhood of great and honorable knights would not care to make the sacrifices required to join—not unless they are simply so jaundiced about how the world has treated them that they think it is the best option they have. The bitterness of this green salad symbolizes the bitter spirit that fills many who join the brotherhood of the black. (*A Game of Thrones*, Chapter 19—Jon)

SERVES 2

3 cups young turnip greens

1 teaspoon salt

3 tablespoons lemon juice

½ cup pine nuts

2 tablespoons olive oil

½ teaspoon garlic powder

½ tablespoon fresh basil

½ tablespoon fresh
   oregano

2 cups diced tomatoes

¼ cup diced green onions

1 cup diced red bell pepper

1. Remove the stems from the turnip greens. Roll up the greens and chop them into small pieces.
2. Sprinkle the salt onto the greens. Massage the greens by hand to work the salt into them so they begin to wilt.
3. Pour 2 tablespoons of the lemon juice on greens and mix. Let them sit for 1–2 minutes to wilt.
4. Blend the pine nuts, olive oil, garlic powder, and remaining 1 tablespoon lemon juice until smooth. Add the basil and oregano to the blender and briefly pulse until the herbs are mixed in but still chunky.
5. Add tomato, onion, and red bell pepper to the turnip greens. Toss the salad with the blended dressing and serve.

A WORD OF WISDOM

Collard greens and kale are two of the most nutrient-rich leafy greens, but turnip greens are even richer in nutrients, so they're better for you. They all belong in same family as cabbage, broccoli, and bok choy.

Southron Spinach and Plum Salad

After a fine day of tourney, Sansa joins the royal court at the riverside for a feast. It's a magical evening where simple joys and the beauty of the night seem all the more enhanced. This salad of spinach and plum is both healthy yet provides a sweetness to complement the flavor of the night for young Sansa, who has no idea how far away such lovely times will seem in the months to come. (*A Game of Thrones*, Chapter 29—Sansa)

SERVES 4

2 cups baby spinach leaves, torn

2 plums, pitted and sliced into wedges

¼ cup balsamic vinegar

¾ cup olive oil

½ cup lemon juice

½ cup orange juice

4 teaspoons lemon zest

4 teaspoons orange zest

¼ teaspoon coarse sea salt

⅛ teaspoon black pepper, ground

½ tablespoon finely chopped fresh basil

1. Arrange the spinach and plum wedges on 4 plates.
2. Whisk vinegar, oil, juices, zests, salt, pepper, and basil in a bowl.
3. Drizzle approximately ⅓ of dressing over spinach and plums on plates. Remaining dressing may be refrigerated.

A Word of Wisdom

Whether you make salad dressing at home or buy it at the store, all salad dressings need to be stored in the fridge and shaken well before each use, unless the recipe or packaging specifically states otherwise.

Cersei's Greens Dressed with Apples and Pine Nuts

Cersei provides a delicious juxtaposition to herself when she serves this simple dish. The complex queen works a web around her enemies at every opportunity; this modest and easy-to-make salad is guileless in comparison. To contrast and balance out the Queen's sometimes cold nature, this dish has a sweet raspberry vinaigrette. (*A Clash of Kings*, Chapter 44—Tyrion)

SERVES 4

2 cups baby greens mix

2 apples, cored and sliced

1 cup pine nuts

¼ cup balsamic or
   raspberry vinegar

2 tablespoons lime juice

¼ cup raspberry preserves

2 tablespoons Dijon
   mustard

½ teaspoon sugar

¾ cup olive oil

Salt and pepper to taste

1. Arrange greens, apple wedges, and pine nuts on 4 plates.
2. Process together vinegar, lime juice, raspberry preserves, mustard, and sugar in a food processor or blender until smooth.
3. Slowly add olive oil, just a few drops at a time, on high speed to allow oil to emulsify. Season generously with salt and pepper.
4. Dress greens with dressing. Refrigerate any leftovers.

A Word of Wisdom

Pine nuts, like peanuts, aren't true nuts, but they're still dangerous to people with some nut allergies. There should be no mystery about what pine nuts really are: they are an edible seed of pine trees!

LORD WALDER'S GREEN BEAN SALAD

Walder Frey offered this salad of green beans, onions, and beets after Late Lord Frey's Leek Soup—possibly the last edible course on a menu that progressed through boiled river pike, jellied calves' brains, and string beef. Vegetarian dish or no, the blood-red beets seem like just one of several signs that coming events would not be feast-worthy. (*A Storm of Swords*, Chapter 51—Catelyn)

SERVES 4

1 pound fresh green beans

4 quarts of water, with a
  pinch of salt

Ice water, to immerse
  beans

2 tablespoons extra-virgin
  olive oil

1 tablespoon lemon juice

1 tablespoon grated
  Parmesan cheese

¼ cup toasted almond
  slices

¼ cup diced red onion

1 roasted beet, cooled and
  thinly sliced (see Cersei's
  Buttered Beets in Chapter
  3 for roasting method)

½ cup cherry tomatoes,
  quartered

Salt and pepper to taste

1. Wash and trim green beans. In batches, blanch beans in pot of boiling water, but only until tender. Remove from boiling water and shock beans (immerse them) in cold water for at least 10 seconds. Remove beans from water and place in a large salad bowl. Repeat until all beans have been blanched and shocked.

2. Drizzle beans with oil and lemon juice. Mix well. Gently toss Parmesan, almonds, onions, beet, and tomatoes into the beans. Salt and pepper to taste. Serve immediately.

A WORD OF WISDOM

Blanching beans locks in nutrition and flavor. Put only small batches of vegetables into the water. You don't want the water to stop boiling, or your vegetables will fade! Cook these beans in handful-size batches until tender.

WUN WEG WUN DAR WUN'S GIANT SALAD

The giants of old were often said to be monstrous, savage creatures that feasted on the flesh of men and children. But Wun Weg Wun Dar Wun is not such a beast: he is quite the picky vegetarian. Inspired by his love for bushels of onions and turnips, one bowl of this delightful salad would be a true treat for Wun Wun; in the cold north beyond the Wall, he's likely not enjoyed the summer greens and tempting southron spices that crows and kneelers so easily take for granted. (*A Dance with Dragons*, Chapter 39—Jon)

MAKES 1 GIANT'S PORTION OR SERVES 4

2 cups romaine lettuce, chopped

1 cup Bibb lettuce, torn

1 cup endive, chopped

½ cup arugula, torn

½ cup red leaf lettuce, torn

⅓ cup sliced celery

¼ cup chopped baby carrots

⅓ cup shredded raw turnip

⅓ cup shredded raw Vidalia onion

4 teaspoons seasoned rice vinegar

¼ teaspoon kosher salt

⅛ teaspoon hot paprika

⅛ teaspoon garlic powder

⅛ teaspoon onion powder

3 tablespoons olive oil

¼ cup grape tomatoes, sliced

WUN WEG WUN DAR WUN'S GIANT SALAD
(CONTINUED)

1. Combine romaine, Bibb, endive, arugula, red leaf lettuce, celery, carrots, turnips, and onions in a large salad bowl. Toss gently to mix.
2. Whisk vinegar, salt, paprika, garlic powder, and onion powder together in a small bowl. Whisk oil into dressing and mix until emulsified.
3. Drizzle dressing over salad. Toss extremely well to coat. Add tomato slices to top of salad as a garnish and serve immediately.

A WORD OF WISDOM

Serve this crisp and refreshing salad before a meal or on its own. The delicate contrasts among greens will end up overpowered by the heavier main dish.

CHAPTER 5

FEASTS FOR FRIENDS— AND ENEMIES:
Main Courses

W hether in Westeros or the lands across the narrow sea, a great feast often foreshadows major events as reliably as a messenger crow's dark wings do. Sometimes these events celebrate the joining of houses in marriage or friendship, where merriment, laughter, and stories are shared over opulent food and drink. Some are war council meetings and last meals before battles, where hasty decisions and the wrong insult may alter the fate of the entire world—and where every dish seems to have a double meaning. And some feasts appear to have one purpose but reveal much darker motivations that often end in disaster and death.

Joyous, serious, or tragic, every gathering must serve food to match. Warriors prepare to fight or die with great roasts in their bellies. Lords drown their sorrows in drink accompanied by auroch, mutton, and duck. Men and women enjoy stuffed birds and honeyed wine as they make plans for the throne or consider how to quietly bring down their enemies. Some will look up from their meals to eye the servants they know to be spies and it's all they can do to enjoy their repast rather than fly into a violent rage. Some warriors in training will mentally pray for the deaths of their enemies while newly wed women may ponder the future of married life and how it may change their worlds. One thing is certain: a grand meal in Westeros is almost never a dull affair and often leads to unexpected results.

WINTERFELL MEATS

When important company arrives at Winterfell, the Great Hall becomes heavy with the smell of roasted meats. As Eddard Stark is forced to smile and greet the Lannisters as his guests, he is also unknowingly marking the end of an era in his life. Though they don't know it, this is the last time the family Stark in its entirety and Jon Snow will be gathered at a table with each other, enjoying themselves and simply being the family of the Warden of the North. It's only fitting to enjoy the finest of Winterfell's noble kitchen as the seasons, their family—and everything else—changes. (*A Game of Thrones*, Chapter 5—Jon)

SERVES 10–12

1 (3- to 4-pound) venison roast or butt, or other roast of choice

¼ cup Dornish Citrus Rub (below)

3–4 tablespoons olive oil

8 ounces mushrooms, sliced

2 cloves garlic, minced

2 turnips, peeled and roughly chopped

3 carrots, peeled and chopped

2 potatoes, peeled and chopped

8 ounces pearl onions

1 can dark beer

1 (10-ounce) can beef consommé

Kosher salt and freshly ground black pepper to taste

Dornish Citrus Rub:

¼ cup dried lemon zest

¼ cup dried lime zest

¼ cup dried orange zest

¼ cup dark brown sugar

1 tablespoon seasoned pepper

Winterfell Meats
(CONTINUED)

1. To prepare Dornish Citrus Rub: Combine all of the ingredients. Set aside ¼ cup for roast. Store the remainder in a glass jar and cover with a tight-fitting lid. This rub will keep for up to 3 months in a dark cupboard away from heat.
2. Sprinkle roast with Citrus Rub. Wrap in plastic wrap and place in a bowl. Refrigerate 8 to 12 hours or overnight.
3. Preheat oven to 350°F.
4. Heat the oil in a deep pan that will hold all of the ingredients. Brown the roast in hot oil. Remove roast from pan and set aside. Add the mushrooms and garlic to the pan. Sauté for 3 or 4 minutes. Add the rest of the ingredients and bring to a boil. Add roast, cover, and place in the oven. Cook for about 1 hour, until meat is fork tender, or until internal temperature reaches at least 140°F. Serve hot.

A Word of Wisdom

Serve your choice of roast with fresh Winterfell Black Bread (Chapter 3), a pint of Direwolf Ale, and a large helping of Arya's Lemon Cakes (both in Chapter 6) for the ultimate Stark-inspired feast.

BRAN STARK'S PIGEON PIE

Though forced to endure a drastic change in his life, Bran Stark can still enjoy a hot pigeon pie while he watches direwolves fight over a bone in the corner. Pigeon is present in many other moments of uncertainty in Westeros, too: a homeless girl sells them in the streets, a king feasts on them moments before his demise, and several curious bannermen eat them while their young lord tries to prove his strength. Despite these somber settings, pigeons seem to represent something hopeful and light—even when fate would cast the future otherwise. (*A Game of Thrones*, Chapter 24—Bran)

MAKES 4 PIES

1½ pounds pigeon breast

½ pound porcini mushrooms

1 bunch green onions

¼ cup (½ stick) unsalted butter

2 tablespoons flour

2 cups heavy cream

4 ounces Boursin cheese

Kosher salt and seasoned pepper to taste

1 roll phyllo dough (4 sheets)

½ cup (1 stick) unsalted butter, melted

Bran Stark's Pigeon Pie

(CONTINUED)

1. Chop the breast meat, mushrooms, and green onions. Melt ¼ cup butter in a pan. Sauté the chopped mixture over medium-high heat for several minutes until meat is cooked. Stir in the flour and cook for 2 minutes. Add cream and cheese and blend well. Season with salt and pepper to taste. Let cool and refrigerate for 4 hours or overnight.
2. Lay out 4 sheets of phyllo on a damp cloth and cover with another damp cloth.
3. Preheat oven to 425°F.
4. Place one sheet of phyllo on a work surface and brush with 1 tablespoon of melted butter. Place one-fourth of the chilled meat mixture on the upper center of the dough. Fold over the sides and roll up. Butter outside of dough heavily. Repeat three times to make remaining pies.
5. Bake for 20 minutes until golden brown and serve hot.

A Word of Wisdom

This dish may be better for feasts than for an everyday dinner, since it needs to partially cook a day ahead. You could also make it, bake it, and freeze it so it is ready to pop in a hot oven when guests are coming. Any game bird can be substituted for the pigeon.

BLACK BROTHER PORK PIE

Menus for the Night's Watch do not include small portions or light options. This pork pie keeps brothers of the black sated and warm while they wait to be called into action— whether they're looking forward to the call or not. The dish is so rich and heavy, anyone who finishes too big a portion may find himself dubbed the Lord of Ham. (*A Game of Thrones*, Chapter 26—Jon)

SERVES 6–8

2 pounds ground pig or boar

2–3 tablespoons olive oil

2 cloves garlic, minced

1 onion, chopped

1 red pepper, chopped

½ cup mushrooms, sliced

4 tablespoons (½ stick) unsalted butter

4 tablespoons all-purpose flour

2 cups chicken broth

2 teaspoons Worcestershire sauce

Kosher salt and pepper to taste

1 (9-inch) unbaked pastry crust

BLACK BROTHER PORK PIE

(CONTINUED)

1. Preheat oven to 450°F. Grease a 2-quart baking dish.

2. Sauté ground meat in olive oil until cooked through and browned. Transfer meat to baking dish. Add 1 more tablespoon oil to pan if needed and sauté garlic, onion, red pepper, and mushrooms until tender, 4 or 5 minutes. Spoon over meat in baking dish.

3. Pour off excess oil from pan. Melt butter and add flour to form a roux (paste). Cook for about 3 or 4 minutes over medium-high heat. Slowly add the chicken broth, stirring to keep smooth. Cook until bubbly and slightly thickened. Remove from heat and add Worcestershire sauce. Season to taste with salt and pepper. Pour over meat and vegetables.

4. Roll out pastry crust to fit over casserole dish. Crimp edges to seal. Prick with a fork to allow steam to escape. Bake until crust is well browned, about 20 to 30 minutes. Serve hot.

A WORD OF WISDOM

You can always serve your preferred pie filling over a trencher—an edible plate—of bread or pastry. Let the ingredients for the filling simmer slowly on the stove for about a half hour, until they are thickened. While they simmer, use a large biscuit cutter to create large crust circles in uncooked pie crust. Bake at 350°F until they are golden brown and crisp. When ready to serve, just spoon the filling over the crust.

DOLOROUS EDD'S PRUNED HEN

Unforgettable for his dark, self-effacing wit, Eddison Tollett always manages to make his comrades-at-arms at the Wall smile with his quirky way of looking at the world. For every compliment he gives, there's sure to be a touch of sardonic humor to follow, and Three-Finger Hobb's cooking isn't spared. Though offended by Hobb's attempt to "prune" him with this dish, Edd likely didn't realize that dried plum and chestnut stuffing is a fairly traditional dish seen from Dorne to the North. Though southron tables might serve a version with thyme, sage, and rosemary, this version would be more familiar to the northmen of the mountain clans. (*A Dance with Dragons*, Chapter 3—Jon)

SERVES 4

4–6 tablespoons chicken broth

1½ cups dried bread cubes

3 slices bacon

¼ cup chopped yellow onion

¼ cup chopped celery

¼ cup chopped carrot

¼ cup chopped prunes

¼ cup roasted and coarsely chopped chestnuts

¼ tablespoon nutmeg

¼ teaspoon cinnamon

¼ teaspoon cloves

Pinch of salt

1 (4-pound) roasting hen, thoroughly cleaned

DOLOROUS EDD'S PRUNED HEN

(CONTINUED)

1. Preheat oven to 375°F. Warm the chicken broth in a small saucepan. Keep warm on low heat while preparing the other stuffing ingredients. Place the bread cubes in a large bowl.

2. Chop the bacon and cook in a large frying pan. Leave the cooked bacon and the fat in the pan and add the chopped onion, celery, and carrots. Cook for 2 to 3 minutes, and add the prunes and chestnuts. Cook until the onion is tender.

3. Add the cooked ingredients to the bread cubes. Stir in the nutmeg, cinnamon, cloves, and salt. Slowly add 4 tablespoons of the warmed chicken broth. Use your hands to shape the stuffing into firm balls roughly the size of snowballs (the stuffing should not be mushy). Add as much of the remaining 2 tablespoons of warmed chicken broth as necessary. Allow all ingredients to cool completely before stuffing hen.

4. To STUFF THE HEN, hold it so that the neck is facing upward, and begin spooning stuffing into the neck cavity. Use skewers to fasten the skin from the neck over the opening. Tuck the wing tips under the back of the bird. Stuff more stuffing into the body cavity of the bird. Tie the legs and tail of the bird together with string to seal the opening. Place hen in a roasting pan.

5. Roast hen for 60 to 70 minutes, basting with its own juices every 15 minutes. Internal temperature at the thigh should register 175°F when done. Allow hen to rest for about 15 minutes before carving.

A WORD OF WISDOM

The fowl you choose to stuff for dinner may not be of the exact proportions this recipe indicates. You'll likely need between ¾ and 1 cup of stuffing for every pound of meat you cook. However, you can always make extra stuffing, cook it separately in a baking pan, and serve it alongside your bird.

GHOST'S CHICKEN

Sometimes appetites are like direwolves, ready to tear into the first chicken they come across. Jon Snow may not be a Stark, but he and his companion Ghost certainly share Eddard Stark's taste for such finely cooked meats. This dish will certainly satisfy the animal within!
(*A Game of Thrones*, Chapter 5—Jon)

SERVES 6

1 (3-pound) chicken
1 Granny Smith apple
1 pear
1 yellow onion
1 carrot
1 stalk celery
½ bulb garlic
½ teaspoon red pepper
  flakes
Kosher salt, to taste
1 tablespoon olive oil
½ cup dry red wine
¼ cup honey
¼ cup cider vinegar
1 cup chicken stock

1. Preheat oven to 350°F.
2. Remove and discard all the skin and visible fat from the chicken. Cut the chicken into serving portions. Core the apple and pear, cut into medium-size wedges, and place in cold water. Peel and cut onion into large wedges. Peel and slice the carrot. Chop the celery and mince the garlic.
3. Season the chicken parts with red pepper flakes and salt. Heat the oil to medium-high temperature in a large Dutch oven. Sear the chicken and vegetables for about 1 to 3 minutes on each side.
4. Add the wine and let reduce by half. Add honey, vinegar, and stock. Drain water from pear and apple, add the fruits to Dutch oven, and bring to a boil. Cover and braise in oven until cooked thoroughly, about 45 minutes or until internal temperature reaches 165°F.

A WORD OF WISDOM

This sweet, tangy, honeyed chicken is braised: it is seared, then cooked in liquid. Pot roasts and meals cooked in slow or pressure cookers are also braised, so the technique may already be familiar.

CRAB OF THE NORTH

The Night's Watch knows well that the sea may provide food when game is scarce in the cold forests of the north. Crab from the Night's Watch stronghold at Eastwatch-by-the-Sea is a wonderful meat that stores well in ice and is easy to prepare. When one faces a lifetime that could be spent in the landlocked Castle Black, crab provides a pleasant escape from Three-Finger Hobb's usual menu. (*A Game of Thrones*, Chapter 21—Tyrion)

SERVES 4

2 tablespoons oil

3 cloves garlic, crushed

1 (1-inch) piece fresh
   gingerroot, crushed

1 stalk lemongrass,
   crushed

2 pounds Alaskan king
   crab legs

1 teaspoon ground black
   pepper

1. Heat the oil in a large pot over medium-high heat.
2. Add the garlic, ginger, and lemongrass; cook and stir until brown, about 5 minutes.
3. Add crab legs and pepper. Cover and cook, tossing occasionally, for 15 minutes. Crab is fully cooked when flesh is pearly and opaque.

A WORD OF WISDOM

If using precooked frozen crab, just place it in the refrigerator overnight to allow it to defrost. You can also wrap it in cling film and place in cold water. Do not use hot water to defrost.

Dothraki Duck

Magister Illyrio served Khal Drogo and his blood riders this honeyed duck on the khal's wedding day. Sweet and filled with fruit, the dish is almost a good wish for the khal's marriage. A touch of spice from Worcestershire sauce would honor Drogo's union with his stormborn dragon. (*A Game of Thrones*, Chapter 11—Daenerys)

SERVES 6–8

3 mallard ducks, or the equivalent of 6 to 7 pounds of duck

3 tablespoons salt, plus kosher salt and freshly ground black pepper to taste

2 apples, quartered

1 orange, quartered

1 cup orange juice

¼ cup dark honey

¼ cup sherry

1 tablespoon Maggi Seasoning Sauce or Worcestershire sauce

2 tablespoons butter

2 tablespoons flour

1. Place ducks in a stockpot and cover with water. Add 3 tablespoons salt, apples, and orange, and bring to a boil. Cook for 45 minutes. Remove from water and place ducks in a pan.

2. Preheat the oven to 375°F. Combine orange juice, honey, sherry, and Maggi. Baste duck with sauce and place in oven for 30 minutes, uncovered.

3. Liberally baste again and add water to pan to prevent duck from sticking. Cover the pan tightly with a lid or cover tightly with heavy-duty foil.

4. Lower heat to 275°F degrees. Roast for 2½ to 3 hours more, depending on size of ducks, basting every 30 minutes. Add water to bottom of pan if dry. Ducks are done when leg joint falls apart; the internal temperature should reach at least 165°F.

5. To make gravy, add 2 tablespoons butter and 2 tablespoons flour to pan juices and cook until slightly thickened.

A Word of Wisdom

Pick the bones clean from this duck! Every shred of meat can be eaten. Use the leftover bits of meat for any of the soups or salads in Chapter 4.

STARK RIB ROAST

The House of Stark eats well when fortunes are good. A cut of red meat worthy of a warrior's feast, an auroch rib roast would have fed a small army—or at least a rotund monarch—quite easily. Make this one with a few cups of Direwolf Ale (Chapter 6) for a full Winterfell flavor. (*A Game of Thrones*, Chapter 22—Arya)

SERVES 8–10

1 (8- to 9-pound) auroch
   rib roast
3 cups dark beer, divided
½ cup dark honey
½ cup balsamic vinegar
2 tablespoons grainy
   German-style mustard
Zest and juice of 1 lime
3 cloves garlic, minced
1 tablespoon kosher salt
1 tablespoon lemon pepper

1. Trim all fat from rib roast and place in a large resealable plastic bag. Combine 1 cup beer, honey, vinegar, mustard, lime zest and juice, garlic, salt, and lemon pepper. Reserve ½ cup of marinade in a covered jar. Pour rest of marinade over rib roast and seal the bag shut. Refrigerate 12 to 16 hours or overnight.
2. Preheat oven to 475°F. Remove roast from marinade and place in a roasting pan. Discard used marinade. Place rib roast in oven and bake for 15 minutes to sear. Add remaining 2 cups of beer to pan.
3. Baste the roast with the ½ cup reserved marinade. Lower heat to 350°F. Continue cooking for about 1 to 1½ hours or until internal temperature registers 140°F for well-done.
4. Let roast rest for 10 to 15 minutes. Bring pan juices to a boil. Season to taste with additional salt and pepper. Carve roast and ladle warm pan juices over each slice.

A Word of Wisdom

You can substitute buffalo for the auroch, as long as you carefully watch the cooking time. Buffalo is very lean and, if overcooked, can become dry and chewy. Cook buffalo to 120°F for rare, 130°F for medium-rare, and 140°F for medium. Overcooked buffalo meat is inedible even to the undead.

Sansa Stark's Fairytale Trout Baked in Clay

Sansa Stark grew up on fairy tales and songs of heroic knights and handsome, noble princes. When she meets Prince Joffrey, she feels like her daydreams are coming true. Fittingly, she is served a fanciful dish of fish baked in a sealed clay pot—a nonsensical menu item perhaps, but one that may foreshadow a future of captivity, not freedom. This version is a little more practical; baked in bread rather than clay, it doesn't require the assistance of a prince to enjoy. (*A Game of Thrones*, Chapter 15—Sansa)

SERVES 8

1 10- to 12-inch round loaf of bread (see A Word of Wisdom)

½ cup freshly grated Parmigiano-Reggiano cheese, plus more to taste

4 large vine-ripened tomatoes, peeled, seeded, and diced

½ teaspoon sea salt

4 cloves garlic, minced

2 teaspoons dried minced onion

1 teaspoon dried parsley

½ teaspoon dried oregano, crushed

½ teaspoon dried basil, crushed

Dried red pepper flakes to taste

Granulated sugar to taste

2 cups cottage cheese, drained

1 large egg

3 cups grated mozzarella cheese

Extra-virgin olive oil as needed

12 ounces of cooked trout, flaked, or any canned seafood of your choice, drained

8 ounces fresh button or cremini mushrooms, cleaned and sliced

Sansa Stark's Fairytale Trout Baked in Clay

(CONTINUED)

1. Preheat the oven to 400°F.
2. Cut the top off of the loaf of bread. Starting about ½ inch from the outer crust, cut a circle around the inside of the loaf, cutting down to about ½ inch from the bottom of the crust; be careful not to pierce it.
3. Remove the soft bread from the inside of the loaf, and use a blender or food processor to make 2 to 3 cups of coarse soft bread crumbs. Mix 1 cup of the bread crumbs with the ½ cup of the freshly grated Parmigiano-Reggiano; set aside.
4. In a small bowl, mix together the tomatoes, salt, garlic, dried onion, parsley, oregano, basil, red pepper flakes, and sugar.
5. In another bowl, mix the cottage cheese with the egg and 1 cup of the mozzarella cheese.
6. Use a pastry brush to liberally coat the inside and the outside of the bread with extra-virgin olive oil. Place the bread crust-side down on a baking sheet. Sprinkle

freshly grated Parmigiano-Reggiano to taste over the bottom inside of the bread.

7. Use a slotted spoon to spoon half of the tomato mixture over the top of the grated cheese; avoid getting too much of the tomato juice in this layer. Spread the cottage cheese mixture over the top of the tomatoes; then spread the trout or seafood over the cottage cheese mixture, and top with the mushrooms. Ladle the remaining tomato mixture and juices over the top of the mushrooms.
8. Sprinkle the remaining mozzarella cheese over the tomato mixture. Sprinkle the bread-crumb mixture over the mozzarella, carefully pressing the mixture down over the cheese. Add more bread crumbs, if desired. Liberally drizzle extra-virgin olive oil over the top of the bread crumbs.
9. Bake for 1 hour, or until the bread crumbs on top are deep brown and the mozzarella cheese underneath is melted and bubbling. Serve immediately.

A Word of Wisdom

Bread like challah lends a sweet flavor to this dish, and because its crust is already soft, it should bake okay if it is just placed on the baking sheet. If you are using bread with an already crusty crust, you may need to wrap the outer crust in foil for the first 45 minutes of the baking time.

Baratheon Boar Ribs with Apple

A king has the luxury of being able to order what he wishes, and after a vigorous hunt it's understandable that he would want a fine boar to consume. While he rides alongside the son he can't quite relate to, King Robert makes sure to demand that such a meal will be ready for him and his knights upon their return. The poor boar, however, is not unlike the rotund king who has seen better days before seeming so tempting of a target for his enemies. (*A Game of Thrones*, Chapter 8—Bran)

SERVES 4

1 fennel bulb, core and brown parts removed, chopped

1 tart apple, peeled, cored, and chopped

½ cup white wine

1 tablespoon butter

½ teaspoon caraway seeds

Salt and pepper to taste

½ cup sour cream (optional)

1 tablespoon vegetable oil

½ cup finely chopped celery

2 tablespoons minced onion

1 apple, peeled, cored, and chopped

2 teaspoons dried rosemary or 2 tablespoons fresh, chopped

½ cup dry bread crumbs or stuffing mix

4 double-thick boar or pork rib chops (7–8 ounces each)

8 wooden toothpicks, soaked in water for ½ hour

Baratheon Boar Ribs with Apple
(CONTINUED)

1. Cook the fennel and apple in the wine, covered, for about 20 minutes. Be sure to keep it wet by adding liquid as needed. Don't let it dry out.
2. When the fennel and apple are very soft, add the butter, caraway seeds, salt and pepper, and sour cream. Stir lightly; then remove from heat. Set aside.
3. Heat the vegetable oil in a skillet over medium heat. Add the celery, onion, apple, and rosemary. Cook about 2 minutes; then mix in the bread crumbs or stuffing mix.
4. Fill the pockets of the chops with the bread-crumb mixture, securing openings with toothpicks.
5. Set the grill to medium and brown chops over direct heat.
6. Place on indirect heat, cover, and grill for about 15 minutes per side. Internal temperature should reach 145°F. Spoon some fennel sauce onto each chop before serving.

A Word of Wisdom

You can either parboil the ribs for 20 minutes, or grill them over indirect heat for about 35 minutes before adding the sauce. Make extra and it will keep in the refrigerator for 2 weeks.

CASTLE BLACK RACK OF LAMB

Celebrations with comrades-in-arms call for the finest meat. The newest brothers of the black enjoy this delicious meal courtesy of the Lord Commander, and even though Three-Finger Hobb serves up a good trencher of stew, this dish would be a rare treat for the boys. Jon Snow—who seems to have the blood of a carnivorous direwolf running in his veins—would particularly enjoy this treat. (*A Game of Thrones*, Chapter 41—Jon)

<u>SERVES 4</u>

Lamb:

2 racks of lamb, about 8 ribs each, well trimmed

Slice of fresh lemon

Salt and pepper

1 cup soft (homemade) bread crumbs

½ cup olive oil or melted butter

2 cloves garlic, minced

2 scallions (both green and white parts), chopped

½ cup Italian flat-leaf parsley, chopped fine

4 fresh sage leaves, shredded, or 1 teaspoon dried sage

Plenty of freshly ground pepper

Mint Sauce:

½ cup (1 stick) unsalted butter

2 teaspoons fresh chives, minced

¾ cup fresh mint leaves, chopped and loosely packed

½ cup white (dry) vermouth

2 tablespoons lemon juice

Salt and pepper to taste

Castle Black Rack of Lamb

(CONTINUED)

1. Rub the lamb with the slice of lemon. Sprinkle the lamb with salt and pepper.

2. Set gas grill on high. If using coals, mound them on one side of the grill basin so that you will provide both direct and indirect heat.

3. Mix together the bread crumbs, oil or butter, garlic, scallions, herbs, and pepper. Depending on the dryness of the crumbs, you may want to add more oil or butter. Set aside.

4. Grill the lamb over direct heat, bone-side down, for 5 minutes. Turn and grill, meat-side down, over direct heat for 5 minutes.

5. Move the lamb to the indirect heat or reduce the heat of the gas grill. With the lamb meat-side up, press the bread-crumb mixture onto the meat. Cover with the lid and roast at about 400°F for 10 minutes. The lamb should be pink on the inside and the crust delicious and crisp. The internal temperature should reach 145°F.

6. To make the mint sauce, heat the butter in a saucepan and add the chives and mint leaves. Add the rest of the ingredients and bring to a boil.

7. Before serving, cut chops apart gently. Serve mint sauce warm in a separate bowl.

A Word of Wisdom

Vermouth has flavorings that wine does not. The recipes are secret, kept in families for hundreds of years. Legend has it that the original recipes were locked away years ago for safekeeping.

LITTLEFINGER'S LAMPREY PIE

If the way to a man's heart is through his stomach, the way to sway Lord Petyr Baelish may be through Lamprey Pie. The tavern standard is his admitted weakness, and he's often willing to spend time with even the most dreadful of people to get a taste. But serving the likes of Littlefinger a dish of eel as slippery as he may not produce the intended consequences . . .
(*A Game of Thrones*, Chapter 33—Eddard)

Flaky Pie Crust

MAKES 1 9-INCH CRUST

1¼ cups all-purpose flour

2 tablespoons sugar

½ tablespoons salt

6 tablespoons butter, cubed and chilled

2 tablespoons lard or vegetable shortening, chilled

2–4 tablespoons ice water

Eel Pie Filling

SERVES 8

2 tablespoons butter

1 large onion, diced

2 stalks celery, diced

2 carrots, peeled and diced

1 bay leaf

1 teaspoon fresh thyme

½ teaspoon salt

½ teaspoon freshly cracked black pepper

3 cups eel or fish stock, divided

½ cup all-purpose flour

½ cup heavy cream

1 pound eel, washed with head and tails removed and cut into 2-inch pieces

LITTLEFINGER'S LAMPREY PIE
(CONTINUED)

1. In a large bowl, sift together the flour, sugar, and salt. Add the chilled fats and rub them into the flour mixture with your fingers until 30 percent of the fat is between pea- and hazelnut-sized, while the rest is blended in well.

2. Add 2 tablespoons of water and mix until the dough forms a rough ball. Add more water, 1 tablespoon at a time, if needed. Turn the dough out onto a lightly floured surface and form a disk. Wrap in plastic and chill for at least 30 minutes or up to 3 days.

3. Remove the dough from the refrigerator about 10 minutes before rolling out. Roll out on a lightly floured surface to a ⅛-inch-thick, 12-inch × 15-inch rectangle, turning the dough often to make sure it does not stick. Dust the surface with additional flour if needed. Place the crust on a baking sheet and chill for 30 minutes before use.

4. Heat the oven to 425°F. In a medium saucepan over medium heat, melt the butter until it foams. Add the onion, celery, and carrots and cook until they begin to soften, about 5 minutes.

5. Add the bay leaf, thyme, salt, and pepper and cook for 3 minutes more, or until the herbs are fragrant.

6. Add 1 cup of the stock and bring to a simmer. Cook, covered, for 10 minutes.

7. In a medium bowl, whisk together the remaining stock, flour, and cream until smooth. Slowly pour it into the simmering vegetables, whisking constantly, and cook until it begins to thicken. Turn off the heat and add the eel. Allow to cool to room temperature.

8. Transfer the eel mixture into a 2½-quart baking dish. Top with the Flaky Pie Crust, tucking the edges of the crust into the pan, and cut 4 or 5 slits in the top to vent steam.

9. Place the dish on a baking sheet and bake for 20 minutes, then reduce the heat to 350°F for an additional 35 to 45 minutes, or until the pie is bubbling and the crust is golden brown. Cool for 30 minutes before slicing.

A WORD OF WISDOM

Want to be prepared the next time you need a lamprey pie (or any other potpie) in a pinch? Double your filling recipe, then cool half and freeze in a large container. When you are ready to use it, just thaw it overnight in the refrigerator. Then all you have to do is prepare a crust, fill, and bake!

OLD BEAR'S HAM STEAK

The Old Bear is a powerful man of simple tastes. Even when he shuts himself away to absorb dark words brought from afar—and considers how best to meet the coming foe—the black brothers ensure that he is never without nourishment. Though it can be a simple breakfast, ham steak can be dressed up well enough to entice even Lord Commander Mormont to abandon worries for a meal's worth of enjoyment. (*A Game of Thrones*, Chapter 70—Jon)

<u>SERVES 4</u>

2 large tart apples, peeled and cored

2 pears, peeled and cored

½ cup white wine

2 tablespoons golden brown sugar

½ teaspoon nutmeg

1 teaspoon ground cinnamon

Juice of ½ lemon and ⅛-inch slice of fresh lemon with peel

1 24–30-ounce thick-cut smoked, precooked ham steak

Caramel Rub:

¼ cup (½ stick) butter, softened

½ cup golden brown sugar

½ teaspoon ground cloves

¼ teaspoon ground nutmeg

1 teaspoon dry mustard

OLD BEAR'S HAM STEAK

(CONTINUED)

1. Coarsely chop the apples and pears. Mix them with the wine, sugar, nutmeg, cinnamon, lemon juice, and lemon slice. Cook over low heat in a saucepan until the fruit is very soft. Remove from heat, and remove the lemon peel before serving. (This can be made up to 2 days in advance and stored in a plastic or glass container, covered, in the refrigerator.) Serve hot or cold with the ham.
2. To make the caramel rub for the ham: In a separate bowl, mix butter, sugar, cloves, nutmeg, and mustard.
3. Press the caramel rub into the ham steak.
4. Prepare the grill for direct heat, on medium. Make sure the rack is well above (9 inches above) the coals or flame.
5. Grill the ham for about 4 minutes per side, letting the caramel rub brown but not blacken. Though precooked, the ham's internal temperature should reach 140°F. Cut the ham in serving pieces and serve with the fruit sauce on the side.

A WORD OF WISDOM

Know your ham before you buy it! Maple and smoked varieties are popular and easy to cook with. But brine-soaked and country hams can be tricky: soaked ham forces you to pay for water weight, and salty country hams need to be soaked before roasting.

BRYNDEN TULLY'S BLACKENED TROUT WITH DORNISH GREMOLATA

What better way to celebrate Brynden "Blackfish" Tully than with a plate full of his name-sake? Grilled trout would likely be a familiar sight on the Blackfish's table. Caught fresh from the clear waters of the Tumblestone, the fish would be a welcome staple in the Riverlands. Pairing it with citrus and peppers like those from Dorne make it fine enough a meal for any noble lord's feast. (*A Game of Thrones*, Chapter 34, Catelyn)

SERVES 4

1 cup orange juice

Zest and juice of 1 lime

Zest of 1 lemon

1 shallot, peeled and
  minced

2 cups peperoncini, finely
  diced

4 (12-ounce) whole trout,
  cleaned

Sea salt and freshly cracked
  black pepper

1. Prepare a medium-hot fire in your grill.
2. Combine the orange juice and lime zest and juice in a bowl. Set aside.
3. To make the Dornish Gremolata: mix together lemon zest, shallot, and peperoncini. Set aside.
4. Rinse trout and pat dry. Season with salt and pepper. Place directly over the grill fire.
5. Grill until the meat is opaque and just beginning to flake when tested with a fork, 8 to 10 minutes per side, turning once about halfway through the grilling time and brushing frequently with the orange-lime baste. Serve garnished with the Dornish Gremolata.

A WORD OF WISDOM

Time your fish well! Most fish cook at 10 minutes per inch of thickness over high heat or 12 minutes per inch over medium heat.

Tyrion's Leg of Lamb

Even when he's in a dire situation and possibly at the mercy of his enemies (which seems to happen often in Westeros), Tyrion Lannister is a man who knows what he wants and doesn't wish to settle for anything less. He understands that dark situations can look brighter even just by thinking of a leg of lamb. And this particular dish is thoroughly distracting: savory garlic and goat cheese mingle with a hint of decadent golden raisins to give this classic castle fare a gourmet twist. (*A Game of Thrones*, Chapter 38—Tyrion)

SERVES 6

1 (6- to 7-pound) leg of
  sheep (see A Word of
  Wisdom)
1 pound spinach leaves,
  roughly chopped
3 garlic cloves, finely
  chopped
2 tablespoons olive oil
¼ cup golden raisins
¼ cup toasted pine nuts
¼ cup fresh basil, chopped
3 ounces soft goat cheese
Kosher salt and freshly
  ground pepper

1. Preheat oven to 350°F.
2. Bone, trim, and butterfly sheep leg. Lay flat.
3. Sauté spinach and garlic in oil over high heat for about 2 to 3 minutes. Place in bowl and stir with the rest of the ingredients. Spread mixture onto the meat. Roll up lengthwise and tie with kitchen twine at 1-inch intervals.
4. Place meat on baking sheet and roast for about 1 hour to desired dryness. Internal temperature should reach 145°F. Let rest for 10 minutes before slicing and serving.

A Word of Wisdom

Lamb is meat prized for its tenderness, and is a common sight in cold storage. Still, peasants are less likely to have lamb: serving mutton gives poorer farmers an opportunity to breed, milk, and shear a sheep before it's used for its meat as well.

SAAN'S MINCED LAMB WITH PEPPER

Exotic pirates like Salladhor Saan enjoy equally exotic dinners. After starting his night with bunches of sweet grapes, he cannot help but dream aloud of jolly tunes that will soon be sung and the fine minced lamb dinner that awaits him. He may be a gruff man who speaks openly of base desires, but after a taste of this dish, no one could fault Saan's lust for food.
(*A Clash of Kings*, Chapter 10—Davos)

SERVES 4

1 tablespoon extra-virgin olive oil

1 large potato, peeled and thinly sliced

1 small eggplant, peeled and sliced

1 pound lean ground lamb

1 large yellow onion, peeled and diced

4 cloves of garlic, peeled and minced

½ teaspoon cinnamon

¼ teaspoon ground cloves

¼ teaspoon freshly ground black pepper

⅛ teaspoon ground allspice

Cayenne pepper, to taste

Salt to taste

½ cup dry red wine

1 (15-ounce) can crushed or diced tomatoes

3 cups low-fat milk

½ cup all-purpose flour

Freshly ground nutmeg, to taste

2 large eggs

1 cup (4 ounces) Gruyère or Swiss cheese, grated

Saan's Minced Lamb with Pepper

(CONTINUED)

1. Use the oil to grease the crock of a slow cooker. Arrange the potato slices over the bottom of the slow cooker, and arrange the eggplant slices on top of the potatoes.

2. Sauté the ground lamb, onion, and garlic in a large nonstick skillet over medium-high heat for 8 minutes or until the meat is browned and the onions are tender. Skim off any fat rendered from the meat and discard. Stir in the cinnamon, cloves, black pepper, allspice, cayenne pepper, and salt, breaking apart the meat as you do so. Stir in the wine and tomatoes; reduce the heat and, stirring occasionally, simmer for 10 minutes or until much of the liquid has evaporated and the sauce has thickened.

3. Transfer the meat mixture to the slow cooker. Cover and cook on low for 3 hours or until the potatoes are cooked through. Meat should reach 160°F to be fully cooked.

4. In a nonstick skillet over medium-high heat, whisk together ½ cup of the milk and the flour to make a paste. Slowly whisk in the remaining milk. Stirring constantly, cook for 10 minutes or until thickened enough to coat the back of a spoon. Remove from the heat and stir in the nutmeg. Whisk the eggs and some of the thickened milk together in a bowl, and then whisk the egg mixture back into the thickened milk sauce. Stir in the cheese.

5. Pour the cheese and milk mixture into the slow cooker. Cover and cook on high for 2 hours or until the topping is firm. Turn off the slow cooker and let the dish rest for 30 minutes before serving.

A Word of Wisdom

An alternative way to make this dish is to start with a third of the cooked meat in the bottom of the slow cooker, add a layer of potato (or use only eggplant, doubling the amount called for and using half of it here), top that with another third of the meat, add the eggplant layer, and top that with the remaining meat.

WINTERFELL MUTTON CHOPS IN HONEY AND CLOVES

Presiding over the harvest feast in the Great Hall of Winterfell, Bran sends a plate of these mutton chops to Meera and Jojen Reed of Greywater Watch. His assumption that the crannogmen don't keep herds of sheep and cattle may be correct; how could herds possibly follow Howland Reed's elusive, floating fortress through swamps, bogs, and quicksand? Sauced with spices that make the meat dance with flavor, this recipe would make anyone feel like he's tasting mutton chops for the very first time. (*A Clash of Kings*, Chapter 16—Bran)

SERVES 4

4 thick loin mutton chops, about 6 ounces each
1 teaspoon ground cloves
2 teaspoons ground cumin
3 tablespoons sweet paprika
2 teaspoons hot paprika
½ teaspoon cayenne pepper
1 teaspoon ground coriander
1 teaspoon orange zest
1 teaspoon sea salt
1 teaspoon freshly ground black pepper

1. Remove the fat from the chops. Mix the rest of the ingredients together in a bowl, then rub the mixture into the chops on all sides. Let the rub permeate the chops for 1–2 hours.
2. Heat the grill to high heat, about 425°F. Grill the chops fast and hot until brown, but do not burn—about 5 minutes per side. Chops should reach 145°F to be fully cooked.
3. Place the chops on a platter to rest for 6 minutes before serving.

A WORD OF WISDOM

Using fresh and freshly ground spices always gives a dish a little something extra. Substitute 1 tablespoon of fresh herbs for every teaspoon of dried herbs in a recipe. If you prefer using a coffee grinder or a mortar and pestle to crush larger, already dried spices like whole cloves, cinnamon, and vanilla, go easy on the seasoning. Freshly ground dried herbs are always more potent than their prepackaged cousins!

BATTLE OF BLACKWATER MUTTON ROAST

Like a lamb before the slaughter, Sansa's innocence seems to lead her into Cersei's clutches at every turn. Sitting captive in Maegor's Holdfast, Sansa waits for news of the Battle of Blackwater along with Cersei's other "guests"—who must stay put or face beheading by Ser Ilyn Payne. To keep up the ruse, Cersei feeds them all as well as ever, this time serving a traditional mutton roast. Few are so careful about their appearances and courtesies as the Queen . . . (*A Clash of Kings*, Chapter 57—Sansa)

SERVES 6

2 large yellow onions

3 stalks celery

3 carrots

½ bulb garlic

1½ teaspoons olive oil

6 mutton shanks

Freshly cracked black
   pepper, to taste

¼ cup crushed tomatoes

½ cup dry red wine

1½ quarts Redwyne Brown
   Stock (see Chapter 4),
   made with lamb or
   mutton

1 bay leaf

2 sprigs rosemary, needles
   only

1. Preheat oven to 350°F. Dice the onions and celery. Peel and dice the carrots. Mince the garlic.
2. Heat the olive oil in a roasting pan over medium-high heat. Season the shanks with pepper, then sear on all sides.
3. Add the onions, celery, carrots, and garlic 1 ingredient at a time, sautéing each for 1 minute before adding next; cook until ingredients are golden and onions are nearly transparent. Then add the wine and let reduce by half.
4. Add the stock, bay leaf, and rosemary; bring to a boil, then immediately remove from heat. Cover and place in oven to braise for approximately 1¼ to 1½ hours, or until internal temperature of mutton reaches 145°F.

A WORD OF WISDOM

A lamb and mutton base for the Redwyne Brown Stock will give this an unmistakable flavor that may not translate for every recipe. Freeze what you don't immediately use for this roast for your next lamb recipe.

Bran's Auroch Joints Roasted with Leeks

Even in the absence of most of the Stark family, Winterfell honors the long summer's last harvest with a feast of epic proportions—with grand servings of meat to match. Spiced and honeyed to perfection, this auroch joint recipe celebrates the hefty cut of cattle. With such an overtly large roast, however, the feast begins to feel like a contrived diversion from Bran's physical disability—rather than a symbol of the house's famed strength. (*A Clash of Kings*, Chapter 16—Bran)

SERVES 8–10

1 (5- to 7-pound) auroch or beef round roast

2 tablespoons olive oil

Kosher salt and seasoned pepper to taste

1 cup dry red wine

1 cup beef consommé

1 bay leaf

3 cups cherry or grape tomatoes, quartered

1 cup Kalamata olives, sliced

1 cup (1 ear) fresh corn kernels

3 tablespoons vinegar

6 tablespoons olive oil

2 cloves garlic, minced

½ teaspoon salt

½ tablespoon sugar

BRAN'S AUROCH JOINTS ROASTED WITH LEEKS

(CONTINUED)

1. Preheat oven to 350°F. Rub roast with oil and season to taste with salt and pepper.
2. Place a Dutch oven over high heat and brown the meat on all sides. Add the wine, beef consommé, and bay leaf and bring to a boil. Transfer to the oven, cover, and bake for about 2½ hours until meat registers 145°F to 150°F, basting several times.
3. Combine tomatoes, olives, and corn in a bowl.
4. In a jar, combine vinegar, oil, garlic, salt, and sugar. Cover with lid and shake to combine. Pour over vegetables and let sit while roast is cooking.
5. When roast has rested for about 10 minutes, cut ½-inch slices about three-quarters of the way through the roast. Spoon vegetable mixture in between slices. Place a piece of foil around the roast to hold the meat and vegetable mixture together. Let stand at room temperature for about 20 minutes. Serve a slice with vegetables per person.

A Word of Wisdom

Bigger animals don't mean tougher meat! Auroch, buffalo, and other cattle actually have the same muscle groups, so the same cuts of meat across different domesticated cattle species will have a similar tenderness.

Bran's Venison Burger

"Winter is coming," but that doesn't mean they stand by and await the darkness. Bran is a determined, resourceful boy filled with a strong resolve in his soul matched only by his curiosity. Inspired by Bran's youth, journeys, and wild heart, this Venison Burger captures a bit of the lighthearted child he trades for a sage wanderer. (*A Clash of Kings*, Chapter 16—Bran)

SERVES 8

2 pounds ground venison

Coarse kosher salt and freshly cracked black pepper to taste

8 or 10 buns, buttered and toasted

1 head romaine lettuce, washed and torn

1 red onion, thinly sliced

2 beefsteak tomatoes, thinly sliced

2 avocados, peeled and sliced

1 cup kalamata olives, chopped

Assorted cheeses, crumbled, sliced, or shaved
(Boursin, Cheddar, blue, pecorino, goat, Monterey jack, etc.)

1 pound bacon, fried crisp

Assorted condiments: mustard, mayonnaise, ketchup, barbecue sauce, etc.

Bran's Venison Burger

(Continued)

1. Form meat into 8 to 10 ¾-inch-thick patties. Place on a baking sheet. Sprinkle with coarse salt and cracked pepper to taste. Turn patties over and repeat the seasoning. Refrigerate for an hour so the meat will hold together on the grill. (Variation: For pan searing, burgers do not need to be refrigerated.)
2. Place breads and buns in a basket.
3. Arrange lettuce, onion, tomatoes, avocados, olives, sliced cheeses, and bacon on a platter. Place crumbled and shaved cheeses in bowls. Set out condiments.
4. Prepare a hot fire in the grill. Sear burgers over high heat for about 2 or 3 minutes per side for medium-rare. Allow internal temperature to reach 140°F for well-done. Place on a platter and serve with all the fixings. A side of Benjen's Roasted Onions or The Dead Man's Roasted Vegetables (both in Chapter 3) may complete this meal.

A Word of Wisdom

Ground venison is very lean, so fat is often added during the butchering process. Give any meatloaf, soups, or chili a new twist with this or another variety of ground game!

Everyman's Skewered Pigeon and Capon

Birds serve many roles in the realm of Westeros. Some deliver messages between the lands. Others offer dreams, visions, and new sight to those like Bran Stark and Orell the wildling. But sometimes, they're simply wonderful food, respected and appreciated at the highest and lowest of tables. This rustic rendition of two commonly enjoyed birds could be found at any tavern or feast table in Westeros. (*A Clash of Kings*, Chapter 16—Bran)

SERVES 6–8

½ teaspoon ground cloves

1 teaspoon dried thyme leaves, crumbled

1 teaspoon dried rosemary leaves, crumbled

½ teaspoon salt

Freshly ground black pepper to taste

6 tablespoons (¾ stick) unsalted butter, softened at room temperature

¾ pound boneless, skinless pigeon breasts

¾ pound boneless, skinless capon breasts

Flour for dredging

Vegetables of your choice—peppers, onions, etc.

Everyman's Skewered Pigeon and Capon

(Continued)

1. In a small bowl, mix together the cloves, thyme, rosemary, salt, and pepper. Using a fork, mash the herbs and spices with softened butter.
2. Cut the pigeon and capon into chunks and dredge with flour.
3. Place the herb-butter mixture on a piece of waxed paper and roll the pigeon and capon in it until evenly coated. At this point, you can wrap the meat in plastic and refrigerate if you want to cook and serve it later.
4. Set the grill to medium or let the coals die to ashes.
5. Thread the meat and vegetables onto skewers, alternating varieties of meat evenly on each skewer. Grill until meat is nicely browned, about 3 minutes, and then turn and grill for 3 more minutes. Internal temperature of meat should reach 165°F.

A Word of Wisdom

Why use unsalted butter? It does not burn as easily as that with salt in it. The cream used in sweet butter is also fresher and of better quality, while salt just acts as a preservative and masks flavors. You can always add salt on your own!

Buttered Quails of King's Landing

After a long day of political maneuvering, Tyrion Lannister enjoys a large meal with Lord Janos Slynt, a meal where every dish has its own wine and could be a full supper on its own. Paired with a glass of Tyrion's favorite Arbor red, this dish of quails drowned in butter would honor any guest with its undeniable richness of flavor. But diners should be wary of drowning themselves—be it in butter, wine, or intrigue masked as hospitality.

(*A Clash of Kings*, Chapter 8—Tyrion)

SERVES 4–6

6–8 quail

1 cup seasoned flour

3–4 tablespoons unsalted butter

2 shallots, finely chopped

¼ cup brandy

2 cups chicken stock

¼ cup almonds, sliced

1 cup sour cream

2 tablespoons horseradish

Kosher salt and freshly ground pepper to taste

1. Dredge quail in flour.
2. Heat butter in a large skillet; add shallots. Sauté the quail on both sides for about 3 or 4 minutes per side along with the shallots until quail is golden brown and crispy.
3. Add ¼ cup brandy and ignite, standing back until flame subsides. Add chicken stock and almonds and bring to a boil. Cover tightly and lower heat to a simmer. Cook for about 1 hour or until leg bones pull off the birds and internal temperature reaches 150°F.
4. Stir in the sour cream and horseradish. Simmer for another 15 minutes.
5. Add salt and pepper to taste, if needed. Serve hot.

A Word of Wisdom

Wild game can be so lean that it needs to have some fat and/ or moisture added while cooking. Many recipes, like this one, often require finishing a sauce or dish with butter or heavy cream—even when they include stocks and milk.

LORDLINGS' GOOSE-IN-BERRIES

The perfect marriage of bird and berry comes just in time for the harvest. Overstuffed and overwhelmed by the harvest feast, Bran sends Lord Cley Cerwyn a dish of this goose in berries to honor House Cerwyn's loyalty to the North. Known well for how easily it pairs with a variety of wines, goose is a fine complement for honored bannermen who work as closely with their liege lord as the Cerwyns do. (*A Clash of Kings*, Chapter 21—Bran)

SERVES 6

2 (about 18 ounces each)
  large goose breast halves
  (partially thawed)
½ cup seasoned flour
6 tablespoons (¾ stick)
  unsalted butter
4 tablespoons blackberry
  jam or Last Bite of
  Summer Blackberry
  Preserves (see Chapter 1)
½ cup heavy cream

1. While goose breast is slightly frozen, carefully slice each breast horizontally into 3 cutlets. Dredge in flour.
2. Melt butter in a skillet and sauté goose cutlets for about 3 minutes per side or until internal temperature reaches 165°F. Set on a plate.
3. Add the blackberry jam to the skillet and melt, stirring. Add heavy cream and stir until beginning to bubble. Add cutlets back to pan to warm. Then serve each cutlet with one-sixth of the cream sauce spooned over the top.

A WORD OF WISDOM

Though crossbreeding of chicken and turkey has left their meat less palatable for some, geese are still usually much like their ancestors: intensely flavored, gamey, dark, fatty, and delicious.

STARK STUFFED QUAIL

It can be difficult when a boy must step into the role of his father, but Bran Stark is stronger than appearances may indicate. While hosting the visiting lords and bannermen, he feasts on stuffed birds and other fine meals. It's a good feast and an educational one. If only he weren't also bothered by such strange dreams . . . (*A Clash of Kings*, Chapter 16—Bran)

SERVES 4–6

8 quail

Salt and pepper to taste

1 package chicken gravy mix

½ cup dry white wine

¼ cup (½ stick) butter

½ cup porcini (Italian brown) mushrooms, brushed and sliced

¼ cup finely chopped sweet onion

½ cup wild rice, cooked

½ teaspoon dried sage leaves or 4 fresh ones, shredded

¼ teaspoon fresh basil

Pinch ground nutmeg

Salt and pepper to taste

4 slices bacon

Watercress, for garnish

STARK STUFFED QUAIL

(CONTINUED)

1. Cut 4 wooden skewers in half, and soak in water for at least a half an hour. Rinse the quail and pat dry. Season with salt and pepper.

2. Make the gravy according to the package directions, adding the white wine. Set aside.

3. Melt the butter in a saucepan and sauté the mushrooms and onions until soft, about 8 minutes. Then add the cooked wild rice and stir in the rest of the ingredients (except the bacon).

4. Set the grill to medium and leave room for indirect heat.

5. Stuff the quail with the mushroom-and-rice mixture. Start with a tablespoon in each quail and pack in more if possible. Close the opening on each quail with wooden skewers. Sear quail for about 2 minutes per side over direct heat.

6. Place the quail breast-side up in a metal or enameled roasting pan large enough to hold the birds without piling them up. Pour the gravy over the quail, then arrange a half strip of bacon over the breast of each quail.

7. Place on the grill, over indirect heat, and close the lid. Roast for 20–30 minutes, depending on the heat of the grill. Grill until brown, or at least 150°F with a meat thermometer. Serve with extra wild rice. Garnish with watercress.

A Word of Wisdom

Quail dry out easily but make a delicate morsel when boned and stuffed. The fresher the bird the better; local hunters may be your best source.

CERSEI'S ROAST SWAN

Whether she is planning her next moves against her enemies or feigning softness and modesty, Queen Cersei keeps up appearances. She never tires of showing off her power and authority, and this dish embodies so much of her presence and authority that it forever recalls Cersei in her full glory. Too often served in its plumage or overflowing with oyster-mushroom stuffing, this spit-roasted version echoes a touch of the Queen's penchant for violence.
(*A Clash of Kings*, Chapter 44—Tyrion)

SERVES 8

2 (4-pound) swans
1½ cups brandy, divided
Coarse kosher salt and
   cracked black pepper to
   taste
1 cup (2 sticks) unsalted
   butter
2 teaspoons thyme
4–6 strips bacon (optional)

1. Lightly coat swans with ½ to ¾ cup of the brandy. Sprinkle inside and out with salt and pepper.
2. Follow manufacturer's rotisserie directions: secure clamp and fork at one end of rotisserie rod, slide rod through center of meat (attaching some of the skin from the front and back of the swans). Attach the other fork and secure clamp. Make sure swans are balanced. Tie up loose wings and legs with string. Rotisserie cook at 300°F over pans of water with the lid closed.
3. Melt butter and add remaining brandy and thyme. Baste swans every 15 to 20 minutes, especially breast meat. If breast meat is getting too cooked, place 2 or 3 slices of bacon over the breast and secure with toothpicks.
4. Swans are done when leg joints begin to move easily and fall apart. Internal temperature in thigh will be about 165°F. Let rest for 10 to 15 minutes and carve.

A WORD OF WISDOM

For a less controversial meal, substitute a large goose. Just double-check that the internal thigh temperature reaches 165°F.

HEARTY BLANDISSORY

Just one course of the seventy-seven at the historic wedding feast, blandissory is a sweet-tart soup of capon boiled in wine. This version is more of a hearty stew—since only the Lannisters are likely to serve a meal of seventy-seven courses—but the fowl is still braised thoroughly in wine. The capon wasn't the only Lannister fledgling done in with wine at that memorable feast, though, so prepare this dish with care. (*A Storm of Swords*, Chapter 60—Tyrion)

SERVES 6

2 yellow onions

1 carrot

1 stalk celery

1 grapefruit

2 oranges

1 lemon

1 lime

1 tablespoon olive oil

3-pound capon

½ cup port wine

¼ cup honey

2 cups Redwyne Brown
   Stock (see Chapter 4),
   made with beef

⅓ cup blanched almonds,
   chopped

1. Preheat oven to 325°F.
2. Cut the onions into wedges. Peel and cut the carrot into quarters. Roughly chop the celery. Quarter the grapefruit, oranges, lemon, and lime (leave the peels on).
3. Heat the oil to medium-high temperature in a large Dutch oven. Sear the capon on all sides. Add the vegetables and fruit; cook for 5 minutes, stirring constantly. Add the wine and reduce by half, then add the honey and stock. When the liquid begins to boil, cover and braise in the oven for 1 hour, or until internal temperature reaches 165°F.
4. Serve the cooking liquid (which will thicken as it cooks) as a sauce accompanying the capon. Garnish with almonds.

A WORD OF WISDOM

If you're making the Redwyne Brown Stock just for this meal, use beef for the most authentic taste. A lamb stock may overpower the other flavors.

Tyrion's Spiced Brawn

Deep in thought over the state of his nephew's wits, Tyrion finds himself enjoying a leche of spiced brawn. This dish's mixture of garlic, apples, peppers, salt, and sugar offers flavors to mimic those of Tyrion's personality. Hot and surprising, yet deep and somehow sweet, this dish is as comfortable on a philosopher's desk as it is in a lord's feast. (*A Storm of Swords*, Chapter 60—Tyrion)

SERVES 6

2 tablespoons brown sugar, packed

1 tablespoon coarse kosher salt

1 tablespoon red pepper flakes

1 tablespoon freshly cracked black pepper

½ teaspoon ground cloves

4 cloves garlic, minced

3–4 tablespoons olive oil

6 apples (crisp and tart varieties like Jonagold)

6 wild pig chops or steaks

1. Prepare a hot fire in a grill. Grease a grill wok.
2. Combine brown sugar, salt, pepper flakes, cracked black pepper, and cloves, whisking to combine. Stir in garlic and olive oil.
3. Core and quarter the apples. Mix together with one-third of the brown sugar mixture. Set aside.
4. Coat the chops with the rest of the brown sugar mixture.
5. Grill chops to 125°F for rare and 135°F for medium-rare; internal temperature should reach 145°F for well-done. While chops are grilling, place apples in a grill wok. Toss with wooden spoons until apples are a bit browned and warmed through. Serve chops in the center of a platter surrounded by the apples.

A Word of Wisdom

Perfect for fall, when the apples are ripe and boars are fat, this dish can be succulent with the perfect combination of tart apples and porcine richness. Substitute wild pig for wild boar or domestic pork in any recipe.

BARRISTAN THE BOLD'S WILD BOAR RIBS WITH DRAGON PEPPER

Forty-seven years after being knighted by King Aegon V, Ser Barristan Selmy still feels the heat of Dornish dragon peppers from this spicy boar dish. First spurned by the Lannisters, then discarded like refuse thanks to a dragon, Barristan is no stranger to the burn of being overlooked, either. Still, his honor ties him to the duty at hand, and his passion for serving his king—or queen—is no less strong than it was the day he first knelt before Aegon the Unlikely. This recipe re-creates that first taste of fire in honor of Barristan's unwavering loyalty.
(*A Dance with Dragons*, Chapter 55—The Queensguard)

SERVES 4

1 tablespoon cayenne
  pepper
2 teaspoons red pepper
  flakes
1 teaspoon ground black
  pepper
1 teaspoon ground fennel
  seeds
1 teaspoon dried thyme
1 teaspoon garlic powder
1 teaspoon paprika
2 teaspoons salt
5–6 pounds baby back ribs
  or spareribs
½ cup vegetable oil in a
  spray bottle

1. Mix all of the dry ingredients together. Wearing rubber gloves (this stuff can burn), rub it into the meat. Cover and refrigerate overnight.
2. Prepare the grill to medium with plenty of room for indirect heat.
3. Grill the ribs over indirect heat for 20 minutes per side, or until temperature reaches 145°F for well-done.
4. Spray with vegetable oil and finish grilling until nicely browned. Serve over polenta with a side of grilled red chilies.

A Word of Wisdom

Very hot peppers can actually burn off your taste buds! If your taste buds are burned, you require more and more hot ingredients in order to taste the spice. Anything subtle will completely escape your taste buds if you're not careful.

SANSA STARK'S BOAR'S RIB

As she attempts to leave behind one way of life and hopes to find another, Sansa Stark makes new allies who offer her an evening's rest with a repast of boar. Many of the ingredients in this recipe must be smashed, bruised, or torn before adding, mirroring the emotional onslaught Sansa has faced on her journey. But in many ways these changes may be nothing more than another set of charades and masks. Add Arya's Lemon Cakes (Chapter 6) to tempt her at dessert, and the dark fantasy will be complete. (*A Storm of Swords*, Chapter 6—Sansa)

SERVES 4

1½ quarts dry red wine such as burgundy

4 bay leaves

1 onion, peeled and sliced

4–6 cloves garlic, smashed, unpeeled

2 ounces Worcestershire sauce

½ cup parsley, rinsed and minced

2–3 whole sage leaves, torn

1 whole lemon, sliced thinly

10 black peppercorns, bruised

5 green peppercorns, pickled

½ cup spicy brown mustard

10 juniper berries, bruised

4 pounds spareribs

1. Mix all ingredients in a large nonreactive (stainless steel or glass) container or bowl. Marinate ribs in mixture in refrigerator for 6–8 hours.
2. Prepare the grill for indirect heat. Remove ribs from marinade. Boil marinade for 10 minutes for food safety.
3. Grill the ribs on low heat for 2 hours or until internal temperature reaches 145°F. Brush with marinade. Then grill an additional 10–15 minutes per side, over direct medium-high heat. Ribs should be caramelized but not burned.

A WORD OF WISDOM

If you wish to make it easier to serve the meat in slices, cook until it has become so tender that when prodded the meat will fall off the bone.

LANNISTER BEEF WITH HORSERADISH

Whatever other faults she has, Cersei Lannister knows her priorities when it comes to the comforts of the body. She understands that an exciting tale can best be listened to when the stomach is fed along with the imagination. This plate of Lannister Beef with Horseradish mirrors the exciting sensations whirling through her mind as she hears a great tale of victory and suspense. (*A Feast for Crows*, Chapter 36—Cersei)

SERVES 8

1 (3-pound) boneless beef
 round rump roast
2 (10¾-ounce) cans onion
 soup
1 teaspoon prepared
 horseradish
1 bay leaf
1 clove of garlic, peeled and
 minced
6 large carrots, peeled and
 cut into 1-inch pieces
3 rutabagas, peeled and
 quartered
4 large potatoes, peeled and
 quartered
1 (2-pound) head of cabbage,
 cut into 8 wedges
2 tablespoons butter
2 tablespoons all-purpose
 flour
Salt and freshly ground black
 pepper to taste
1 cup sour cream, optional

1. Cut the beef into eight serving pieces and add it along with the soup, horseradish, bay leaf, and garlic to a slow cooker. Add the carrots, rutabagas, potatoes, and cabbage wedges. Cover and cook on low for 8 hours or until the internal temperature reaches 145°F.
2. Remove meat and vegetables to a serving platter, discarding bay leaf; cover platter and keep warm.
3. Increase the slow cooker setting to high; cover and cook until the pan juices begin to bubble around the edges. Mix the butter and flour in a bowl together with ½ cup of the pan juices; strain out any lumps and whisk the mixture into the simmering liquid in the slow cooker. Cook and stir for 15 minutes or until the flour flavor is cooked out and the resulting gravy is thickened enough to coat the back of a spoon. Taste for seasoning and add salt and pepper if desired. Stir in the sour cream if using. Serve alongside or over the meat and vegetables.

A WORD OF WISDOM

If you prefer a more intense horseradish flavor with cooked beef, increase the amount to 1 tablespoon. Taste the pan juices before thickening with the butter and flour mixture, and add more horseradish at that time if desired.

MERMAN'S COURT VENISON WITH ROASTED CHESTNUT

In leading a double life to pacify his enemies and protect his allies, Lord Wyman Manderly serves the Freys a lovely meal of Merman's Court Venison with Roasted Chestnut in his opulent Merman's Court. It is a noble dish, but it's apparent to anyone who can see beyond the simple but remarkable repast that there may be something more prickly going on. (*A Dance with Dragons*, Chapter 29—Davos)

SERVES 4

1 pound chestnuts

2 tablespoons olive oil

1 cup coarse kosher salt

¾ teaspoon freshly cracked black peppercorns

¾ teaspoon freshly cracked green peppercorns

4 venison chops or steaks, or other big game

1 stick unsalted butter, softened

2 tablespoons shallots, finely chopped

1 tablespoon tarragon vinegar

1 tablespoon chopped fresh tarragon

½ tablespoon fresh Italian parsley, chopped

¼ teaspoon kosher salt

¼ teaspoon hot sauce

1. Preheat oven to 400°F. Cut an X into each chestnut on the flat side.

2. Place on a baking sheet and bake for 30–35 minutes, turning frequently. Peel while warm.

3. Prepare a hot fire in the grill. Combine salt and cracked peppercorn in a small bowl.

4. Rub olive oil on meat and sprinkle with salt and peppercorn. Set aside.

5. Combine remaining ingredients and stir to blend. Place into a ramekin. Set aside.

6. Grill meat for about 3 to 4 minutes per side for rare to medium-rare; for well-done, the internal temperature should reach 140°F.

7. Serve venison and chestnuts with a pat of the butter mixture on top.

A WORD OF WISDOM

When butchering elk, venison, or other big game, have the round steak, skirt steak, or flank steak cut into small (4- to 6-ounce) portions and run through the meat cuber once or twice to tenderize. The meat will be very tender and tasty and will cook quickly.

Northern Roast Elk

Feasting nobles and scavenging wanderers consider elk a true prize for its taste. A challenge to bring down, as Varamyr Sixskins can attest, elk are all the more respected, coveted, and satisfying for the chase. (*A Dance with Dragons*—Prologue)

SERVES 10–12

1 (5- to 7-pound) elk
  tenderloin
2 tablespoons olive oil
Kosher salt and cracked
  black pepper to taste
4 tablespoons (½ stick)
  butter
3 shallots, finely chopped
3 tablespoons hoisin sauce
2 tablespoons Dijon
  mustard
½ teaspoon freshly ground
  black pepper
1 cup sherry

1. Preheat oven to 500°F.
2. Coat tenderloin with oil and liberally sprinkle with salt and cracked pepper. Place in a shallow pan and roast for 5 minutes per pound. Then turn off oven, but do not open the oven door. Keep in the oven for 10 minutes per pound for rare tenderloin (i.e., 50 minutes for a 5-pound tenderloin, and 70 minutes for a 7-pound tenderloin). If meat is too rare after that time, turn the oven on to 375°F and cook for another 15 to 20 minutes to desired doneness. Well-done elk should reach an internal temperature of 140°F. Let rest for 10 minutes.
3. In a saucepan, melt the butter and sauté the shallots. Add the rest of the ingredients. Bring to a boil and reduce heat to a low simmer to keep warm. Spoon over carved tenderloin and serve extra on the side.

A Word of Wisdom

Big-game tenderloins and roasts can be quite large. Butcher large tenderloins in half or to desired weight for cooking smaller portions and to avoid any waste. Keep tenderloins and roasts to 4 to 5 pounds for best results in roasting, grilling, and braising.

PYKE ONION PIE

After years spent dreaming of his home and his position of power there, Theon Greyjoy suffers quite a rude awakening when faced with the reality of the Iron Islands. Nothing works as he had planned, and familiar faces are more likely to mock him than welcome him. The one small comfort he finds is an onion pie served at his father's feast. That a simple pie is the only thing on Pyke that doesn't disappoint bodes poorly for Theon. (*A Clash of Kings*, Chapter 24—Theon)

SERVES 8

3 strips thick-cut bacon, chopped

3 large, or 4 medium, yellow onions, peeled and sliced ¼-inch thick

2 teaspoons sugar

½ cup water

3 cloves garlic, minced

1 teaspoon apple cider vinegar

¼ teaspoon fresh grated nutmeg

1 teaspoon hot sauce

1 recipe Blitz Puff Pastry (see Chapter 6)

1 egg, beaten

1 cup shredded Gruyère cheese

¼ teaspoon smoked paprika

PYKE ONION PIE

(CONTINUED)

1. In a large sauté pan over medium heat, cook the bacon until crisp. Remove the bacon from the pan and allow to drain. Reserve the fat.
2. Add the onions and sugar to the pan, and cook for 1 minute. Reduce the heat to medium-low and add ¼ cup of the water. Cook, stirring constantly, until the onions are well caramelized, about 30 minutes. If the pan becomes too dry or the onions begin to stick, add the additional water.
3. Once the onions are caramelized, add in the garlic, vinegar, nutmeg, and hot sauce and cook for 1 minute. Remove from the heat and allow to cool.
4. Heat the oven to 425°F and line a baking sheet with parchment paper.
5. Roll out the pastry to ⅛-inch thick, then use a pizza wheel to cut out a 12-inch circle. Place on the prepared baking sheet and brush the edge of the pastry with beaten egg, creating a border of about ½ inch. Fold this ½-inch in to create a rim. Poke several holes in the center of the pastry, cover with plastic, and chill for 30 minutes.

6. Once pastry is chilled, spread the caramelized onions over it. Top with the cooked bacon and the shredded cheese, and dust the top with the paprika. Bake for 15 minutes, then reduce the heat to 350°F and bake for an additional 30 to 40 minutes, or until the pastry is crisp and golden. Serve warm.

A WORD OF WISDOM

To ensure your baked goods cook as evenly as possible, rotate them halfway through cooking to promote even browning. You can also place a pizza stone or unglazed tiles on the bottom rack to help even out the heat.

DORNISH WHISKERFISH

At a macabre, fairy-like feast, a prince and a white knight dine in the highest fashion. Along with long green peppers and capons, Dornish Whiskerfish graces the table. Even cooked, the creature is so large that four men struggle to bring it to the table. But smaller whiskerfish from the Greenblood river would make just as keen an impression at a smaller celebration.
(*A Dance with Dragons*, Chapter 38—The Watcher)

SERVES 4

4 (7-ounce) catfish fillets

½ cup sun-dried tomatoes, chopped

½ cup cured olives, chopped

¼ cup fresh basil, chopped

2 tablespoons extra-virgin olive oil

1 lemon, quartered

1. Preheat oven to 350°F.
2. Rinse fish and pat dry. Place fillets in a casserole dish.
3. Combine sun-dried tomatoes, olives, basil, and olive oil in a bowl. Stir to blend. Spread about 2 to 3 tablespoons of the relish over each fish fillet.
4. Cover the casserole with foil and bake in the oven for about 15 minutes. Uncover and bake for another 5 minutes or until fish is done (when it is opaque and just begins to flake when touched with a fork). Serve fillets with any extra relish and a wedge of lemon.

A WORD OF WISDOM

It goes without saying that the best-tasting catfish is going to come from clean streams and lakes. Because they are bottom feeders, the meat may taste muddy. It's best to fish for catfish before the water temperature gets too warm. When cleaning the fish, remove any of the meat that has blood in it, keeping only the firm white flesh.

LANNISTER HERB-CRUSTED PIKE

To please a queen is a rare and powerful feat to accomplish within a lifetime. As she considers her victory and looks forward to other plans coming to fruition, Cersei celebrates her pleasure with several dishes, including herb-crusted pike. Likely caught where the Blackwater Rush collides with the salty Blackwater Bay, this carnivorous fish suits the ruthless Queen well. (*A Feast for Crows*, Chapter 24—Cersei)

SERVES 4

½ cup flour

1 cup saltine cracker
   crumbs

1 teaspoon salt

1 teaspoon black pepper

½ teaspoon sage leaves,
   dried and crumbled

½ teaspoon oregano, dried

¾ cup fresh parsley, finely
   chopped, divided

4 (7-ounce) pike steaks

½ cup vegetable oil or
   more, divided

4 tablespoons (½ stick)
   butter

3 lemons, halved

1. Combine the flour, cracker crumbs, salt, pepper, sage, oregano, and ½ cup of the parsley in a bowl. Dredge the fish in the flour mixture and place in a single layer on a baking sheet.
2. Heat a large skillet with ¼ cup of the vegetable oil.
3. Over medium-high heat, sauté the fish steaks in batches for about 3 or 4 minutes per side, until opaque, cooked through, and golden brown. Remove from pan and keep warm. Add more oil as necessary for sautéing.
4. Drain excess oil and place skillet over medium heat. Add the butter and melt, stirring with the pan drippings until combined.
5. Plate the fish, squeeze 1 lemon over all, and top with the remaining parsley. Then drizzle the butter over all. Serve with additional lemon halves.

A Word of Wisdom

Pike can be bony, but larger fish are easiest to fillet. Just caution your guests to be careful when they dig in!

Eastern Fire Crab

East of the Reach and King's Landing, just north of Kingswood and the Wendwater, tide ebbs and flows out of Blackwater Bay, pulling with it whatever life (or death) finds its way there. Here, crabs of excellent flavor can be found. When the tide recedes, Davos claims several Blackwater crabs as a meal. This exotic recipe might be well known to spice smugglers, like Ser Davos, running both coasts of the narrow sea and testing their goods along the way. (*A Storm of Swords*, Chapter 5—Davos)

SERVES 4

2 tablespoons vegetable oil
1 teaspoon turmeric powder
½ teaspoon black mustard
  seeds
2 green cardamom pods,
  bruised
2 cloves
8 fresh curry leaves
1 large red onion, finely
  chopped
1 teaspoon grated fresh
  gingerroot
1 pound crab on the shell
Table salt to taste
1 teaspoon red chili powder
¼ teaspoon turmeric powder
1 teaspoon coriander
  powder
1 (14-ounce) can light
  coconut milk

1. In a large skillet, heat the vegetable oil. Add the turmeric, mustard seeds, cardamom, and cloves. As soon as the spices begin to sputter, add the curry leaves, onions, and gingerroot; sauté for 7 to 8 minutes or until the onions are well browned.
2. Add crab and stir well. Cook until the crab is pearly and opaque.
3. Reduce heat. Add the salt, red chili powder, turmeric, and coriander powder; sauté for 1 minute. Add the coconut milk and simmer for about 15–17 minutes, or until curry thickens. Don't let the coconut milk boil. Spoon sauce over the crab as you cook, making sure it is completely basted.

A Word of Wisdom
Crabmeat is tastiest when freshly cooked, but can be stored for a couple of days in the refrigerator before the taste starts to truly be affected. Frozen, it can remain good for about four months.

Pentoshi Crisp Fingerfish

Across the narrow sea, east of King's Landing, Dragonstone, and Claw Isle, lies the port city of Pentos. Known for its fishing, Pentos is one of the Free Cities where the scent of spices and fish dishes can be smelled all around. Partake of Pentoshi Crisp Fingerfish and the rest of the world may melt away—including the kingdoms across the narrow sea locked in battle for the sake of an iron chair. (*A Dance with Dragons*, Chapter 1—Tyrion)

SERVES 4

About 5 cups oil, for deep-frying

1½ pounds fresh fingerfish, haddock, or cod fillets

4 large egg yolks

3 cups bread crumbs

2 fresh lemons

1. Add the oil to a large, heavy saucepan, wok, electric fondue pot, or deep-fat fryer. Heat the oil to 350°F. Be sure to follow the manufacturer's instructions for deep-frying with the specific appliance.
2. Rinse the fish fillets and pat dry with a paper towel. Cut the fillets into finger-length strips. Beat the egg yolks.
3. Place the fish strips, beaten egg yolks, and the bread crumbs near the stove. Lay paper towels on a plate and keep near the stove for draining the fish strips.
4. Dip each fish strip into the beaten egg, and then coat with the bread crumbs. Deep-fry the fish according to instructions, making sure the fish is completely submerged. Drain the deep-fried fish on the paper towels.
5. Cut each lemon into wedges, and serve as garnish with the fish.

A Word of Wisdom

Fish are commonly classified based on their fat content. Lean fish such as red snapper and halibut have a fat content under 3 percent. At the other end, oily fish like swordfish, salmon, and tuna have a fat content of over 10 percent. Lean fish are often sautéed or baked, while broiling is a good cooking method for fish with a higher fat content.

KHALEESI'S HEART

Though she is barely a child in Pentos, Daenerys finds herself thrown into adulthood and making choices she never would have dreamed she would make. In possibly the most vivid and alien moment of her life to date, she proves her strength and loyalty to Khal Drogo's khalasar by eating a great stallion's still-beating heart—a practice many other cultures frown on as barbarism. This recipe emulates the Dothraki tradition with fiery grilled beef heart. Unnerving to some and thrilling to others, this dish could prove almost anyone's mettle. (*A Game of Thrones*, Chapter 46—Daenerys)

SERVES 10

4 fresh aji amarillo chilies (if you prefer this dish more mild, remove seeds)

5 cloves garlic

1 tablespoon water, if needed

3 tablespoons cumin

1 teaspoon salt

1 teaspoon pepper

1 cup red wine vinegar

2 cups vegetable oil, divided

1 beef heart, cleaned and cut into very thin 2-inch squares

KHALEESI'S HEART

(CONTINUED)

1. In a food processor, purée aji amarillo chilies and garlic until they form a paste. Add up to a tablespoon of water if needed to get a paste texture. Place in a large resealable plastic bag with cumin, salt, pepper, vinegar, and ½ cup of the oil. Close bag and mix marinade gently with your hands.

2. Place beef heart into bag. Close bag and mix to thoroughly cover heart with marinade. Refrigerate overnight.

3. When ready to cook heart, prepare a very hot fire on grill. Soak several bamboo skewers in water for at least 30 minutes; you'll need enough to fit all of the strips, so assume at least 10.

4. Thread 4 strips of heart onto each skewer, making sure each strip lays flat. The skewer should go through each piece twice.

5. Reserve the marinade in a small pot and carefully bring to a boil for three minutes. Allow to cool, then add remaining oil.

6. Lay skewered heart on grill and baste generously with marinade-oil mix. Cook skewers for no more than 2 minutes on each side. This meat is best served medium-rare. Turn and baste continuously.

7. Serve immediately.

A WORD OF WISDOM

There is much debate about the marinating time for this dish. Some complain that the meat is too tough if marinated overnight in vinegar; other swear by it. Decide for yourself, and experiment! As long as the slices are very thin and cooked very quickly, the meat should stay deliciously tender.

DECEITFUL DELIGHTS:
Desserts, Drinks, and
"Poisonous" Cocktails

D essert is too often taken for granted, but not in Westeros and
the lands across the narrow sea. There, sweets are for royalty
and those of noble blood. Sugar is not a product in common
use, and for peasants, too much in one dish would be an extravagance to
serve—unless good, hard-earned coin brought it to the table. In the Seven
Kingdoms, dessert is served to those who are born into wealth and privi-
lege, but it is not so for others less fortunate. Arya Stark's beloved treats
become a thing of the past when her life takes a quick turn, and her lemon
cakes are then just a memory of a taste she won't find in most street markets. Tarts abound at feasts, but are absent on long, hard journeys.

However, not everything sweet is a dessert. Spirits are tied to the
progression of every day, of every emotion in life. Wines, stouts, and ales
may all be bought or brewed to suit guests' tastes and to complement the
manifold dishes of the land.

Still, these temptations have their consequences. Many assassins and
wily killers have found ways to turn these appetizing amusements into
deadly weapons. Poisons and venoms are discovered hidden in food and
drink—even on the blade of a weapon—but always too late for the poor
victim. Assassins treasure their poisons as much as Jaime prizes his sword
hand, and the alchemy-inspired concoctions in this chapter reveal truths
about the devious poisoners that keep the game of thrones ever-changing.

For your pleasure, these recipes help a meal stand apart from the rest
and mark the tables they're served on as owing fealty to great houses—
and great treasures. Whatever you desire to inspire your taste buds and
quench your thirst, from desserts Lannisters and Starks could agree on as
delicious to signature brews from across the Seven Kingdoms, this chapter is sure to accommodate you.

Arya's Lemon Cakes

Despite her youth, Arya is one of the most strong-willed and determined characters when we first meet her. But as her sister Sansa is aware, the youngest Stark girl does have one weakness: lemon cakes. Just a mention of them can distract the free-spirited Arya from her impulse to defy orders and conventions—if only for a few moments. To Arya, the cakes represent happy times at home, something worth selling street-caught pigeons for when times are tough. (*A Game of Thrones*, Chapter 15—Sansa)

MAKES 10–12 SMALL CAKES

1½ cups warm milk

1 teaspoon granulated sugar

1¾ teaspoons active dry yeast (1 package)

1 egg

¼ teaspoon lemon verbena oil or lemon extract

2 tablespoons unsalted butter

½ teaspoon kosher salt

1 cup all-purpose flour

2 tablespoons dried lemon verbena, crushed

ARYA'S LEMON CAKES

(CONTINUED)

1. In a large bowl, mix milk, sugar, and yeast. Set aside for about 10 minutes, until foamy.
2. Mix in egg, lemon verbena oil, 1 tablespoon of the butter, salt, flour, and dried lemon verbena. Beat together 5 minutes until a smooth dough is formed.
3. Cover with plastic wrap and rise in a warm spot for about 1½ hours (until doubled in volume).
4. Heat griddle over high heat. Test by sprinkling on a little water. If griddle sizzles and water evaporates, it's ready.
5. Lower heat to medium-low. Melt remaining tablespoon of butter on the griddle. Place muffin rings on griddle and fill halfway with batter. Cover loosely with foil and cook until cakes are browned on the bottom, about 5 minutes.
6. Using spatula or tongs, flip over each small cake and ring. Cover and cook another 5 minutes. Serve warm.

A WORD OF WISDOM

Muffin or crumpet rings will keep your cakes thicker and compact. If you don't have any handy, you can cut open both ends of short, metal food cans—like those used to pack tuna. Remove the labels and wash them very thoroughly. When you're ready to make lemon cakes, flour the inside well then use them instead of muffin rings.

Arya's Apricot Crumb Tart

When familiar resources and support are nowhere to be found, life in the city becomes dangerous and guided by instinct. Arya's stomach is gnawed by hunger and the smell of nearby foods becomes intoxicating, overriding other priorities. This impractical desire forces her into a practical solution. As she catches a pigeon, Arya prays she might be able to trade it for even something as small as an apricot tart. Such a treat would bring a welcome break from the growing emptiness in her stomach. (*A Game of Thrones*, Chapter 65—Arya)

Short Crust

MAKES 1 (10-INCH) TART CRUST

¼ cup sugar
1 stick unsalted butter, slightly softened
1 egg yolk
½ teaspoon vanilla
1⅓ cups all-purpose flour

Butter Crumble Topping

MAKES ENOUGH CRUMBLE FOR 1 PIE

½ cup all-purpose flour
½ cup sugar
¼ teaspoon salt
⅓ cup unsalted butter, cubed and chilled

Pie Filling

SERVES 8

4 apricots, peeled, pitted, and cut into ½-inch
  slices
¾ cup packed light brown sugar
¾ tablespoon cornstarch
2 tablespoons heavy cream
¼ teaspoon salt
½ teaspoon cinnamon
¼ teaspoon mace
½ teaspoon vanilla
2 tablespoons butter, melted and cooled

ARYA'S APRICOT CRUMB TART

(CONTINUED)

1. TO PREPARE CRUST: Cream together the sugar and butter until just combined. Add in the egg yolk and vanilla and mix well.
2. Add in the flour and mix until the dough is smooth. Wrap in plastic and chill for 1 hour or up to 3 days.
3. Remove dough from the refrigerator for 10 minutes to warm up. Roll out on a lightly floured surface to a ⅛-inch-thick, 12-inch circle, turning the dough often. Dust the surface with additional flour if needed.
4. Roll the dough around the rolling pin and unroll it into a 10-inch tart pan, pressing the dough into the pan. Press your fingers against the rim of the pan to trim the dough. Cover with plastic and chill until ready to bake.
5. TO PREPARE CRUMBLE: Blend the flour, sugar, and salt in a medium bowl. Using your fingers, rub in the butter until the mixture resembles coarse sand. Chill the crumble for 30 minutes before use.
6. Heat the oven to 375°F.

7. In a large bowl, combine the apricots, light brown sugar, cornstarch, cream, salt, cinnamon, mace, vanilla, and butter. Gently toss until the fruit is evenly coated.
8. Arrange the apricots in the prepared crust and spread the Butter Crumble mixture evenly over the top. Place the tart on a baking sheet and bake, in the lower third of the oven, for 40 to 50 minutes, or until the crumble is golden brown and the tart is bubbling. Cool to room temperature before serving.

A WORD OF WISDOM

To best tell if apricots are ready to eat, first look for plump, bright orange fruit. Discard any that are pale yellow or white. Second, test for softness. The fruit should just give under slight pressure. Finally, smell them. A strong apricot smell is an indication that they are ripe and ready.

SANSA'S STRAWBERRY CHIFFON PIE

A young dreamer like Sansa cannot help but giggle and gossip with a friend about the dealings of the royal court at King's Landing. As she shares secrets, romanticizes the knights she's seen, and ponders why some things seem not to fit into the fairy tales she grew up with, her mood is made all the better by sharing a strawberry pie with a friend. One bite of this dish will chase away serious thoughts, leaving only smiles and the desire for girlish laughter. (*A Game of Thrones*, Chapter 44—Sansa)

Traditional Graham Cracker Crust

MAKES 1 (9-INCH) PIE CRUST

1⅓ cups graham cracker crumbs

3 tablespoons sugar

6 tablespoons unsalted butter, melted

Pie Filling

SERVES 8

1 quart fresh strawberries, hulled and quartered

¾ cup sugar

3 tablespoons cornstarch

¾ cup cranberry juice

Stabilized Whipped Cream

MAKES TOPPING FOR 1 (9-INCH) PIE

½ teaspoon unflavored powdered gelatin

1½ teaspoons cold water

1 cup heavy whipping cream, cold

3 tablespoons powdered sugar

1 teaspoon vanilla

SANSA'S STRAWBERRY CHIFFON PIE

(CONTINUED)

1. TO PREPARE CRUST: Heat the oven to 350°F. Combine the graham cracker crumbs, sugar, and butter in a medium bowl until well combined. Press the mixture evenly into a 9-inch pie pan. Bake for 10 to 12 minutes, or until the crust is golden brown and the center is firm when pressed lightly. Cool completely before filling.

2. In a medium bowl, combine half of the strawberries with the sugar. With a potato masher or a fork, mash the berries until mostly smooth. Stir in the remaining berries and let stand for 10 minutes.

3. In a large saucepan, combine the berry mixture, cornstarch, and cranberry juice. Cook over medium heat until the mixture thickens and bubbles.

4. Pour the mixture into the prepared, cool crust and chill for 4 hours.

5. Once chilled, prepare the Stabilized Whipped Cream. In a small bowl, mix the powdered gelatin with the cold water. Let stand 10 minutes, then melt in the microwave for 10 seconds. Allow to cool for 5 minutes, or until cool to the touch.

6. In a medium bowl, add the cream, powdered sugar, and vanilla. Whip with a stand mixer or with a hand mixer on medium-high speed until it starts to thicken. Slowly pour in the cooled gelatin and whip until the cream forms medium peaks.

7. Spread whipped cream over the top of the pie. Chill for 30 minutes before serving.

A WORD OF WISDOM

Fresh strawberries will retain some of their texture after cooking. Frozen berries will be too mushy.

THE VALE SUMMER BERRIES AND CREAM TART

The eastern sky is rose and gold as the sun rises over the Vale of Arryn, where reputedly impregnable Eyrie stands tall and secure. Lulled into complacency, the people of the Eyrie celebrate and make merry, even when it seems that enemies are rising against them. A tart of summer berries and cream this good may be worth forgoing reality for just a little while. (*A Game of Thrones*, Chapter 40—Catelyn)

Blitz Puff Pastry

MAKES 1 TART CRUST

1⅓ cups all-purpose flour

1 tablespoon sugar

¼ teaspoon salt

1½ sticks unsalted butter, cut into 1-inch pieces and chilled

6 tablespoons ice water

Tart Filling

SERVES 8

8 ounces cream cheese, room temperature

½ cup confectioners' sugar, plus more for garnish

1 teaspoon vanilla

1 teaspoon lemon zest

½ cup fresh strawberries, hulled and sliced

½ cup fresh blueberries

½ cup fresh raspberries

½ cup fresh blackberries

¼ cup apricot jelly

A WORD OF WISDOM

If you want, you can transform your large tart into individual tarts very simply. First, cut the dough into 4-inch circles. Divide the filling among the circles, fold, and bake. You will need to check the tarts starting at 20 minutes to avoid overcooking. Individual tarts are great for bake sales, tea parties, and cocktail parties.

THE VALE SUMMER BERRIES AND CREAM TART
(CONTINUED)

1. In a large bowl, combine the flour, sugar, and salt. Mix well. Add the chilled butter and blend it into the flour mixture with your fingers until 10 percent of the fat is blended in well, leaving the rest as very large chunks, between hazelnut and pecan size. Add the water a little at a time and mix the dough with a spatula until it just hangs together. It will look very shaggy.

2. Turn the dough out onto a well-floured surface. Shape the dough into a rectangle and roll it out to ½-inch thick. Dust the top with additional flour if the butter is too soft, but do not add too much. Use a bench scraper or a large spatula to fold the dough into itself in thirds, similar to folding a letter. It will be crumbly.

3. Turn the dough 90 degrees and square off the edges of the dough. Roll the dough into a rectangle that's ½-inch thick. Brush off any excess flour from the dough and fold the dough in thirds. Repeat this process two more times, then wrap in plastic and chill for 30 minutes.

4. Remove from the refrigerator and allow to stand for 10 minutes. Roll the dough out into a ½-inch-thick rectangle, dust off any excess flour, then fold the 2 shorter sides into the center and then in half at the seam, like a book. Roll out the dough to ½-inch thick, wrap in plastic, and chill for 1 hour before use.

5. Heat the oven to 400°F and line a baking sheet with parchment paper.

6. Roll the pastry out to ½-inch thickness and trim into a 12-inch square. Place the pastry on the prepared baking sheet and pierce with a fork. Top the pastry with a second sheet of parchment paper, and then place a second baking sheet on top of the pastry.

7. Bake for 12 to 15 minutes, or until the pastry is firm. Remove the top baking sheet and parchment paper and bake for an additional 12 to 15 minutes, or until the pastry is golden brown and crisp. Allow to cool completely to room temperature.

8. In a medium bowl, beat the cream cheese with the confectioners' sugar, vanilla, and lemon zest until fluffy and smooth. Carefully spread the cream cheese mixture over the pastry, leaving a 1-inch border around the edge. Arrange the fruit on the cream cheese.

9. In a small saucepan, melt the apricot jelly until thin. With a pastry brush, glaze the fruit with the melted jelly. Dust the edges of the pastry with confectioners' sugar, if desired.

SAMWELL'S BLUEBERRY RICOTTA TART

When Samwell Tarly was growing up in the Reach, many tried to make him into something that he wasn't. He was given weapons and told to fight, but Sam preferred the company of books and fine-tasting food. These daydream-worthy Blueberry Ricotta Tarts are just the kind of thing he ate as he pursued his passions and shirked his lordling duties. (*A Game of Thrones*, Chapter 26—Jon)

SERVES 8

1 cup ricotta cheese
2 teaspoons lemon zest
1 teaspoon vanilla
2 tablespoons honey
2 tablespoons sugar
1 egg yolk
¼ teaspoon salt
1 (12-inch) round pastry
  crust, chilled
1 cup fresh blueberries
½ recipe Butter Crumble
  Topping (see Arya's
  Apricot Crumb Tart
  recipe in this chapter)

1. In a large bowl, whisk together the ricotta, lemon zest, vanilla, honey, sugar, egg yolk, and salt. Cover and chill for 30 minutes.
2. Heat the oven to 350°F and line a baking sheet with parchment paper or lightly grease the sheet.
3. Place the chilled pastry onto the prepared baking sheet. Spread the ricotta mixture onto the pastry, leaving a ½-inch border. Arrange the blueberries over the ricotta mixture, then fold the pastry just over the edge of the filling. Top with the Butter Crumble Topping.
4. Bake for 45 to 55 minutes, or until the fruit is bubbling and both the crumble and pastry are golden brown. Cool to room temperature before serving.

A WORD OF WISDOM

Parchment paper is a wise purchase—baked goods won't stick and it makes cleanup quick and easy. You'll find parchment readily available in the foil section of the supermarket.

RICKON'S APPLE CAKE

In Westeros, life can change to death suddenly, and one has to be quick, strong, and smart to stay safe, but little Rickon is too young to do much more than follow his would-be saviors or captors—or worse. He enjoys an apple cake while others plan his future for him. Children of any age would be easily entertained by this homey dessert, and it might even tempt them into (or out of) safety. (*A Clash of Kings*, Chapter 69—Bran)

SERVES 8–10

3 cups all-purpose flour

2 cups sugar

1 teaspoon baking soda

2 teaspoons pumpkin pie spice (or cinnamon)

1 teaspoon salt

1¼ cups vegetable oil

3 eggs, beaten

2 teaspoons vanilla extract

5–6 heirloom apples, peeled, cored, and chopped

1 cup nuts, chopped (pecans, black walnuts, or English walnuts)

1. Preheat oven to 375°F.
2. Combine flour, sugar, baking soda, pumpkin pie spice or cinnamon, and salt. Stir to blend. Stir in oil, eggs, and vanilla extract (mixture will be dense). Stir in apples and nuts. Pour batter into a 9-inch springform pan and bake for about 75 minutes or until the top of the cake is crusty and dark brown.
3. Remove from oven and let cool for 15 minutes. Run a knife around the edges of the cake before releasing it from the springform pan. Cake will keep for several days at room temperature.

A Word of Wisdom

Interesting heirloom apples are finding their way into orchards and farmers' markets. Try a medley of heirlooms like Doctor Matthews, Holiday, Keepsake, Rome, or White Winter Pearmain. If none are available, substitute Jonathan or Red or Golden Delicious.

TOMMEN'S BAKED APPLE CHEESE TART

As wars rage on and tragedies occur, Cersei becomes more and more brittle from the realization that none of her plans are working out correctly, and she begins to fall into the overindulgence of food and drink that King Robert was known for. But the Queen is not as concerned for herself as she is for her children, and she considers both her enemies and how to deal with them as she spies young Tommen eating an apple tart. (*A Feast for Crows*, Chapter 12—Cersei)

SERVES 8

1 recipe Blitz Puff Pastry (see The Vale Summer Berries and Cream Tart, steps 1–4, in this chapter)

1 egg, beaten

6 strips thick-cut bacon, chopped

¼ cup apple butter

6 ounces Brie cheese, cut into ¼-inch slices

2 Granny Smith apples, cored, and sliced ¼-inch thick

2 tablespoons freshly grated Parmesan cheese

TOMMEN'S BAKED APPLE CHEESE TART
(CONTINUED)

1. Heat the oven to 400°F and line a baking sheet with parchment paper or lightly grease the sheet.

2. Roll the uncooked pastry out to ½-inch thick and trim into a 12-inch square. Place the pastry on the prepared baking sheet. Brush the beaten egg along the edge of the pastry, leaving about a ½-inch border. Fold the edges of the pastry in, making a ½-inch lip around the edge of the pastry. Using a fork, pierce the center of the pastry. Cover with plastic and chill for 30 minutes.

3. In a medium skillet over medium heat, cook the bacon until it just begins to brown. Remove from the pan and drain well.

4. Spread the apple butter over the center of the puff pastry. Arrange the Brie cheese, apples, and bacon over the apple butter and dust the top with Parmesan cheese.

5. Bake for 30 to 40 minutes, or until the pastry is golden and the apples are tender. Cool for 5 minutes before serving.

A WORD OF WISDOM

Brie is a cow's milk cheese that is allowed to age and ripen for as little as a few months to as long as a few years. Brie is best when served at room temperature and can also be baked. Brie baked in a pastry crust is called brie en croute. *Jam, fruit, and crackers are popular accompaniments for the soft cheese.*

BITTERBRIDGE BLACKBERRY TART

At his house's seat of Bitterbridge, Lord Caswell serves an unforgettable meal to powerful and influential characters whose decisions will change the fate of the Seven Kingdoms in unpredictable ways. Such guests must be suitably fed, and blackberry tarts are a welcome side dish. You may enjoy them yourself as a fun dessert to share with friends as you discuss what you think of the events at Bitterbridge and what followed. (*A Clash of Kings*, Chapter 22—Catelyn)

SERVES 8

1 Short Crust for tarts, unbaked (see Arya's Apricot Crumb Tart, in this chapter)

8 ounces cream cheese, room temperature

2 tablespoons sour cream

¼ cup sugar

1 teaspoon lemon zest

1 teaspoon vanilla

2 tablespoons all-purpose flour

Blackberry Topping:

2 cups fresh blackberries

⅓ cup sugar

¼ teaspoon vanilla

1 teaspoon fresh lemon juice

2 tablespoons cornstarch

2 tablespoons water

BITTERBRIDGE BLACKBERRY TART
(CONTINUED)

1. Heat the oven to 350°F. Line the tart with parchment paper or a double layer of aluminum foil and add pie weights or dry beans. Bake for 12 minutes. Remove the paper and weights and bake for an additional 10 to 15 minutes, or until the crust is golden brown all over. Remove from the oven and set aside to cool. Leave the oven on.

2. In the bowl of a food processor or stand mixer, mix the cream cheese, sour cream, sugar, lemon zest, vanilla, and flour. Process until very smooth. Refrigerate until ready to bake.

3. TO MAKE BLACKBERRY TOPPING: In a medium saucepan, combine the blackberries, sugar, vanilla, and lemon juice. Cook over medium heat until the berries have softened, about 10 minutes.

4. Combine the cornstarch with the water and stir into the berry mixture. Cook until thickened, about 3 minutes, then remove from the heat and set aside to cool.

5. Remove the cheese mixture from the refrigerator and spread it into the prepared crust. Place the tart pan on a baking sheet and bake for 30 to 35 minutes, or until the cheese mixture is lightly golden and puffed all over. Cool to room temperature, then spread the blackberry mixture on top. Chill for 1 hour before serving.

A WORD OF WISDOM

It may be tempting to try to warm up cold butter or cream cheese in the microwave to save time. Taking the time to slowly soften ingredients will ensure that they are uniformly softened. Microwaving can create hot pockets within the ingredient or warm it too much, ruining your creation. Take the time to do it right, warming at room temperature about 1 hour, because it is worth it!

CELEBRATORY PEACHES IN LAVENDER HONEY

Sansa Stark was locked into a life-altering event that filled her with fear and dread day in and day out. But after an unexpected change, she finds herself free once more and her delight is nearly overpowering. She rejoices with a sweet dish of Peaches in Lavender Honey, a simple, elegant, rich dish befitting her birth and youth. (*A Clash of Kings*, Chapter 65—Sansa)

SERVES 4

4 ripe peaches
½ cup brown sugar
4 tablespoons lavender
  honey
¼ cup chopped walnuts
¼ teaspoon grated ginger

1. Preheat oven to 350°F.
2. Cut the peaches in half and remove the pits. Sprinkle the brown sugar over a nonstick baking pan. Lay the peach halves on top of the brown sugar.
3. Drizzle the honey over the peach slices. Sprinkle walnuts and ginger evenly over them.
4. Bake the peaches for 15 minutes or until tender. Let cool briefly, and serve while still warm.

A WORD OF WISDOM

True lavender honey is produced by bees that have access only to lavender nectar, but you can make lavender-infused honey at home. Just mix 6 tablespoons of fresh lavender buds and 4 cups of honey in a saucepan. Heat over medium until honey feels warm, then set temperature as low as possible for 30 minutes. Pour into hot, sanitized Mason jars. Seal in a water-bath canner for 15 minutes. (See Last Bite of Summer Blackberry Preserves in Chapter 1 for more about this canning method.)

King's Landing Blood Melon Sorbet

Farmers bring a variety of fruits to King's Landing—large, sweet, oblong blood melons included. Even when Eddard Stark knows that danger lies around him and dark times wait ahead, such smells and food can bring a sense of comfort and serenity. This cool, summery treat might have given him pause if he'd stopped to find one, but the unmistakably foreboding omen is still tied well to the name. (*A Game of Thrones*, Chapter 27—Eddard)

MAKES 1 QUART

3 cups blood melon juice
  or watermelon juice (see
  step 1)
⅔ cup sugar
1 tablespoon freshly
  squeezed lemon juice
¼ cup mini chocolate
  chips (for "seeds")

1. Remove the melon flesh from the rind, taking care to discard seeds. Purée in food processor or blender until smooth.
2. Place the sugar and 1 cup of melon juice in a small pot and stir over medium heat until all of the sugar is dissolved. Allow to cool and then combine with the lemon juice and remaining melon juice. Cover and refrigerate until cool.
3. Add to ice-cream maker and follow manufacturer's instructions for freezing. Add in chocolate chips toward the end of freezing. Remove from freezer 10–15 minutes before serving to ensure that it's soft enough to eat.

A Word of Wisdom

Cut the melon in half rather than smaller chunks before removing the flesh. Take extra care when scooping out the flesh so that you make a large "bowl" out of one half of the rind. Once the sorbet has gone through the churn cycle, pour it into the melon bowl to freeze.

QUEEN OF MEEREEN'S PERSIMMON CRUMBLE ICE CREAM

Closeted in her Meereenese pyramid, Daenerys sits and listens and waits—for her enemies' next move, for Drogon's return, for the next betrayal. Bored and frustrated by the Qartheen merchant prince Xaro Xhoan Daxos, Dany can't help but imagine his nose as a persimmon. Honoring her rare moment of levity and her guest's unforgettable visage, this dessert would offer relief from ennui, worry, and heat for any young queen. (*A Dance with Dragons*, Chapter 2—Daenerys)

MAKES ABOUT 1 QUART

3 cups heavy cream
1 cup sugar
1 teaspoon vanilla extract
1 cup persimmon pulp, chilled
1 cup crumbled butter cookies

1. Combine cream, sugar, and vanilla extract. Pour into ice-cream maker and begin to freeze according to manufacturer's directions.
2. After 5 minutes, add the persimmon pulp. Continue freezing. After another 5 minutes, add the crumbled butter cookies. Finish freezing the ice cream, then serve.

A WORD OF WISDOM

Wild persimmons are ready to eat after the first hard frost. Pick them when they are mushy. It is fairly easy to squeeze the seeds and the pulp apart. If using store-bought persimmons, try to find Hachiyas. They soften when they are ripe and are preferable to Fuyus, which are crunchy like an apple.

BALLROOM BLACKBERRY HONEYCAKE

One event after another sours Sansa Stark's life, so much so that she may wonder if she's cursed by the gods (both old and new) for some twisted amusement. But a life with such trials should be balanced with some sweetness. Sansa takes blackberry honeycakes as a form of comfort in the Queen's Ballroom. The berries are oddly symbolic of Sansa's predicament. Once caught in blackberry brambles—so seemingly innocent—their thorns will only dig deeper into the traveler who tries to press forward; the only way out is back. (*A Storm of Swords*, Chapter 59—Sansa)

SERVES 8

¼ cup (½ stick) butter, softened

¼ cup honey

1 egg, beaten

1 cup flour

1½ teaspoons baking powder

⅓ cup plain yogurt

1 teaspoon vanilla

2 cups blackberries, sweetened to taste with honey or sugar

½ cup raw sugar

¼ cup (½ stick) butter, softened

⅓ cup flour

1. Preheat oven to 350°F. Grease and flour an 8-inch or 9-inch cake pan.
2. In a large mixing bowl, cream butter and honey. Add beaten egg.
3. In a separate bowl, combine flour and baking powder. Add to creamed mixture.
4. Fold in yogurt and vanilla.
5. Pour batter into prepared cake pan. Cover with sweetened blackberries.
6. To make the topping, cream the sugar and butter. Stir in flour until mixture is crumbly. Sprinkle crumb topping over blackberries.
7. Bake for 45 minutes.

A WORD OF WISDOM

This summery crumb cake could be made with any berry to take full advantage of a stolen, peaceful moment.

White Harbor Hippocras

North of the Saltspear, Barrowton is the seat of House Dustin. Here, Roose Bolton meets and plans with others while feasting on White Harbor's finest imported fare. Casks of hippocras would sweeten any negotiation quickly—thanks to the overwhelming sugar and fine red wine used to make it. (*A Dance with Dragons*, Chapter 32—Reek)

MAKES 2 PINTS

2 pints red wine, your choice

1 pound sugar

4 tablespoons ground cinnamon

6 tablespoons ground ginger

½ teaspoon ground black pepper

1. Pour wine into a large pitcher or bowl.
2. Add sugar and spices to wine. Stir well, dissolving as much sugar as possible.
3. Cover container of wine securely, and allow to infuse. Taste often to determine when infusion meets your expectations. The longer you infuse the wine, the stronger the spiced taste. Infusion should be complete within 7 days.
4. Strain liquid through cheesecloth four times to separate out all spices.

A Word of Wisdom

Dreamwine from Qarth is also an infused wine. While the exact ingredients are foreign to most Westerosian palates, you can choose your own exotic ingredients to create an equally intoxicating blend. Strong flavors may only take a few days to infuse, but delicate flavors will take longer. Always strain your infused wines well to keep them smooth.

Cersei's Plum Wine

It's been said that wine brings out the truth in people. For Queen Cersei, it's a tool that can bring a sheltered person courage to face the truth. She even keeps flagons of this variety at the ready for her double-edged purposes. Fermented from fruit that likely grew in orchards nourished by the Blackwater, this plum wine might be easy enough for anyone to make, but only the Queen could boast of having the finest. (*A Clash of Kings*, Chapter 60—Sansa)

10–12 WINE BOTTLES

3 pounds wild plums
1½ gallons water
4 pounds sugar
1 teaspoon wine yeast
2 Campden tablets

1. Wash, stem, and pit the plums. Cut them into small pieces, reserving the juice. Crush well and put into a 5-gallon crock or large sterilized bucket, adding enough water to cover plums. Put a lid, muslin, or cheesecloth over the top and let stand for 24 hours.
2. Strain the plums through the cloth and return the juice to the crock. Add the sugar and yeast. Cover and let stand for 4–5 days.
3. Stir each day and skim the foam off the top.
4. Strain the juice. Add enough water to make 2 gallons. Put in gallon jars with airlocks and rubber stoppers in place. Let stand 2 weeks.
5. When the fermentation is complete, use plastic tubing to siphon the wine into sterilized bottles. Cork and rack for at least 3 months. Siphon wine into a bottling bucket (known as racking) and add Campden tablets according to the manufacturer's instructions. Bottle and cork wine immediately. Age for 6 months to 1 year before drinking.

A Word of Wisdom

To make your own wine, you'll need:

+ *A large crock (2–5 gallons), bucket, or one-gallon glass jars*
+ *Cheesecloth or muslin to cover the container*
+ *An airlock for the secondary fermentation*
+ *A small hose or plastic tubing for siphoning wine*
+ *Wine bottles with corks to siphon the wine into*

STARK SPICED WINE

In the halls of Winterfell, the kitchen staff does what it can to bring warmth to the people of the North. When winter clouds are gathering, even a young man with a name such as Jon Snow can find himself craving warmth. This hot, spiced wine warms the chest and the blood with a hint of southron flavors. (*A Game of Thrones*, Chapter 5—Jon)

MAKES 20 DRINKS

1 cup sugar

4 cups water

Spiral of lemon peel

18 whole cloves

2 cinnamon sticks

2 750-ml bottles red dinner wine

1. Dissolve sugar in water in large saucepan. Add slices of lemon peel, cloves, and cinnamon. Boil 15 minutes.
2. Strain out the peel and spices. Add the wine and heat gently, but do not boil.
3. Serve in stemmed mugs.

A WORD OF WISDOM

The ironborn might prefer glögg, a similar drink. Just heat (do not boil) 2 bottles of wine, 1 tablespoon of cognac, ½ cup fine sugar, 5 whole cloves, and 2 cinnamon sticks and serve with a side of slivered almonds and raisins.

STAG STRONGWINE SNIFTER

"Ours is the Fury!" The motto of the House Baratheon and its sigil, the great stag, make it clear that Baratheons are a passionate people, embracing primal emotion. Robert Baratheon certainly fits the bill, a large man with large desires, especially for strongwine. This cocktail, inspired by the power and flavor of the renowned spirit from the Arbor, is sure to have the power to sate any great man—and to fell him as quickly as its namesake does. (*A Game of Thrones*, Chapter 47—Eddard)

1 SERVING

1 ounce cognac
1 ounce Grand Marnier

Pour ingredients into a brandy snifter and serve.

A WORD OF WISDOM

Cognac is twice-distilled wine. Grand Marnier is a liqueur made of blended cognacs and bittersweet orange. Both boast an alcohol volume of 40%, and the combination is classic.

TEARS OF LYS

The deadliest and stealthiest of all poisons, tears of Lys is as rare as it is untraceable—the perfect choice for the discerning assassin. This cocktail isn't quite as lethal as its namesake, but is doubtless a poison worth picking. Cachaça is the perfect spirit for the job: not only is it made from fermented sugarcane juice; home distillers can formulate blindingly strong batches that are more potent than whiskeys and vodkas. The lime hints at its exotic and mysterious origins, and simple syrup further belies this drink's dark purpose. One sip can erase any lingering doubts about why it so easily catches its victims off-guard . . . (*A Game of Thrones*, Chapter 30, Eddard)

MAKES 1
LETHAL SERVING

1 lime, quartered
1 teaspoon simple syrup,
  purchased or made by
  dissolving 1 part sugar in
  1 part warm water and
  cooling
2 ounces cachaça or white
  rum

1. Place a lime wedge and the simple syrup in an old-fashioned glass and muddle well.
2. Add the cachaça and stir well.
3. Fill the glass with ice and stir again.

A WORD OF WISDOM

Not every drink is best served with muddled fruit and ice. If you prefer a clear, unadulterated cocktail, mix the whole drink in a Boston shaker, shake to combine, and strain the liquid out into your glass. Purists may argue that shaking "bruises" the spirit, but what's a little bruising between poisoners?

THE STRANGLER

In the halls of Dragonstone, elderly Maester Cressen finds his lord in dire circumstances and decides to take action. Desperate, he prepares to use the strangler, a rare amethyst-colored poison known well by the Citadel and favored in political assassinations. This cocktail is nowhere near as dangerous as Cressen's brew, but it still has a good kick. (*A Clash of Kings*, Prologue)

MAKES 1 DRINK

1 ounce blueberry
   schnapps
2 ounces cranberry juice
½ ounce lemon-lime soda

1. Pour blueberry schnapps and cranberry juice into a Collins glass over ice.
2. Stir, then top with the soda.

A Word of Wisdom

The color of your strangler may differ depending on the exact color of liquids you use.

MANTICORE VENOM

Manticores are built for killing: the legendary beast has the body of a lion, the head of a human, teeth like a terrible shark, and a scorpion's tail. Its venom is a delicate and potent poison. Oberyn Martell relies on its subtle yet ruthless effects. This regal but powerful cocktail recipe is merely inspired by the venom, and is nowhere near as deadly . . . nor does it need to be wrested from any beast, real or imagined. Like thickened manticore venom, the true nature of this drink may take time to reveal itself. (*A Storm of Swords*, Chapter 70—Tyrion)

MAKES 1 DRINK

1 ounce chilled peach
   purée
Prosecco sparkling wine
   to fill
1 peach slice for garnish
   (optional)

1. Pour the peach purée into a champagne flute and fill with Prosecco.
2. If desired, garnish with a peach slice.

A Word of Wisdom

The best purées for cocktails have a little sugar added. Blend 1 peach and 1 tablespoon sugar until fully puréed. Then press the purée through a fine sieve to remove any large solids. Store in an airtight container in the refrigerator for no more than a week.

HOUSE OF BLACK AND WHITE'S GOLDEN COIN

From the House of Black and White, there comes a small someone with an ugly little girl's face, and she is not someone to bargain with. Her hands are illusive weapons. Even something as simple as a coin may cost her victims more than they'd imagine. Inspired by the deadly deception, this gold-filled shot could lay out a grown man if delivered correctly, so it's not for the faint of heart nor health. (*A Dance with Dragons*, Chapter 64—The Ugly Little Girl)

MAKES 1 SHOT

Goldschläger
Chilled spiced rum

Into a shot glass, layer the ingredients in order with a spoon.

A WORD OF WISDOM

The differing densities of spirits keep them floating separately. Using a spoon to add them slowly may not improve the taste, but will keep the presentation flawless.

CRANNOGMEN'S POISON

In the swamplands of the Neck, the crannogmen live entrenched in bogs and mashes filled with curiosities and dangers. They may be smaller than many other warriors in Westeros, but they are no less formidable or cunning, often tipping their arrows with poison to kill quickly from a distance. Murky and green as the land that hides Greywater Watch, this shot of liqueurs can sneak up on just about anyone. (*A Clash of Kings*, Chapter 21—Bran)

MAKES 1 DRINK

1 ounce green crème de menthe

1 ounce white crème de cacao

2 ounces cream

1. Pour the green crème de menthe, white crème de cacao, and cream into a shaker tin of ice.
2. Shake and strain into a cocktail glass.

A Word of Wisdom

Neither crème de menthe nor crème de cacao have dairy products in them, unlike cream liqueurs that do include dairy cream and must be stored more carefully.

PYROMANCERS' WILDFIRE

Tyrion Lannister understands the tactical advantages of firepower and knows just how nasty the pyromancers' wildfire can be. Legendary for killing the Targaryen prince Aerion Bright-flame when he drank it, wildfire burns hot and fast, consuming everything it touches. This flaming drink takes its name, color, and presentation from the infamous weapon of war, shining green and making any who are brave enough to try it feel sure they, too, could have a drop of dragon blood in their veins. (*A Clash of Kings*, Chapter 20—Tyrion)

MAKES 1 DRINK

½ ounce green crème de menthe

½ ounce gold tequila

⅛ ounce Grand Marnier

1. Pour the green crème de menthe into a shot glass.
2. Gently pour the gold tequila over the back of a spoon to layer it on the crème de menthe. Repeat with the Grand Marnier.
3. Ignite the drink. Be sure to blow out the flame before trying to drink it.

A Word of Wisdom

The Alchemists' Guild takes extreme precautions when handling their wildfire, and you should take equal care when handling yours. Close all open bottles of alcohol before you ignite the shot. Don't add alcohol if the shot is actively burning. Use sturdy glasses to prevent cracking and shattering—or you will have a very wild fire on your hands!

BLACKWATER SCHWARZBIER

Tyrion Lannister may have enjoyed this drink in Winterfell, but its name points southeast to King's Landing, which resides beside Blackwater Bay. With a surprisingly light body and clean finish, this smooth beer complements the fine, comfortable climes of the eastern shore and is proof that dark doesn't mean strong, bitter, or acrid. (*A Game of Thrones*, Chapter 9—Tyrion)

FOR 5.5 GALLONS AT 1.052, 31.6 SRM, 22.6 IBUS, 4.9 PERCENT ABV; 90-MINUTE BOIL

Malt/Grain/Sugar

9.00 pounds Vienna Malt

1.00 pound Munich Malt (Dark)

0.50 pound Crystal 60L

0.75 pound Carafa II Dehusked Chocolate Malt

Extract (for 8.00 pounds of Vienna Malt)

5.50 pounds Munich Liquid Malt Extract (LME)

Hops

0.50 ounce Hallertauer Mittelfruh (4.5 percent AA) Pellet for First Wort

Hopping

0.50 ounce Tettnanger (4.5 percent AA) Pellet for 60 minutes

0.50 ounce Hallertauer Mittelfruh (4.5 percent AA) Pellet for 20 minutes

Other Ingredients

1 tablet Whirlfloc

1 tablespoon Yeast Nutrient

Yeast

Wyeast 2206 Bavarian Lager/WLP830 German Lager

BLACKWATER SCHWARZBIER

(CONTINUED)

Mash Schedule

Intermediate Rest 120°F 20 minutes
Saccharification Rest 152°F 60 minutes

Follow the Multistep Brew Process (see Appendix A).

A Word of Wisdom

Munich malt has the flavor of a rich, dark bread. In comparison, its cousin Vienna malt tastes more like a toasted cracker. Use Vienna when you want a beer that's snappy, but still malty. If you prefer your Blackwater Schwarzbier already bottled, look for brews like Samuel Adams Black Lager, 10 Barrel S1N1STOR, Buckbean Black Noddy Lager, or Sprecher Black Bavarian.

BITTERSWEET VOLANTENE STOUT

Ser Jorah Mormont is not the sort of traveling companion a certain dwarf desires, and the disgraced knight knows it. But he has a duty to follow and missions to complete, and he will not waver from them. In Volantis, he enjoys a bittersweet stout as he considers the future and is on guard for nearby enemies. This drink is rich and creamy with a smooth coffee-chocolate flavor, one that comforts the body as much as Jorah wants his loyalty to comfort the queen he serves. (*A Dance with Dragons*, Chapter 27—Tyrion)

FOR 5.5 GALLONS AT 1.052, 43 SRM, 28 IBUS, 5.1 PERCENT ABV; 60-MINUTE BOIL

Malt/Grain/Sugar
8.00 pounds Maris Otter Ale Malt
1.00 pound Oat Malt (or Flaked Oatmeal)
1.00 pound Crystal 150L
0.75 pound Roasted Barley
4.00 ounces Black Patent Malt

Extract (for 7 pounds of Maris Otter Malt/Mild Malt)
5.5 pounds Pale Liquid Malt Extract (LME) (Maris Otter Preferable)

Hops
0.5 ounce Target (10.0 percent AA) Pellet for 60 minutes
1.0 ounce Fuggle (4.5 percent AA) Pellet for 20 minutes

Other Ingredients
1 tablet Whirlfloc

Yeast
Wyeast 1318 London III

BITTERSWEET VOLANTENE STOUT

(CONTINUED)

Mash Schedule

Saccharification Rest 153°F 60 minutes

Follow the Single-Infusion Brew Process (see Appendix A).

A WORD OF WISDOM

If you choose to use flaked oatmeal rather than oat malt, remember to steep with a pound of pale malt to convert the starches in the oatmeal. For a ready-made brew similar to Bittersweet Volantene Stout, try Santa Cruz Ale Works Dark Night Oatmeal Stout or Ninkasi Brewing Company Oatis Oatmeal Stout.

DIREWOLF ALE

It is said that giants helped Brandon the Builder construct Winterfell. One sip of Direwolf Ale would have anyone wondering if the giants taught Brandon to brew, too. This drink has a bite like the Starks' direwolf and has a chill that sings of coming winter. A welcome treat on cold nights, this deep brew is the kind kept on hand for long hours over pints and feasts of savory roast meats. (*A Game of Thrones*, Chapter 5—Jon)

FOR 5.0 GALLONS AT 1.097, 16.4 SRM, 28 IBUS, 9.6 PERCENT ABV; 120-MINUTE BOIL

Malt/Grain/Sugar
10.00 pounds Golden Promise/Maris Otter Ale Malt
2.00 pounds Toasted Pale Malt (see A Word of Wisdom)
0.67 pound Crystal 80L
0.67 pound Wheat Malt
1.00 ounce Roasted Barley
1.00 ounce Peat Smoked Malt (optional)
3.00 pounds Pale Liquid Malt Extract

Extract (for 9 pounds of Maris Otter Malt)
8.0 pounds Pale Liquid Malt Extract (LME) (Maris Otter Preferable)

Hops
1.0 ounce East Kent Goldings (6.5 percent AA) Pellet for 60 minutes
1.0 ounce East Kent Goldings (6.5 percent AA) Pellet for 45 minutes

Other Ingredients
1 tablet Whirlfloc

Yeast
Wyeast 1728 Scottish Ale/White Labs WLP028 Edinburgh Ale

Direwolf Ale

(CONTINUED)

Mash Schedule

Saccharification Rest 154°F 60 minutes

Follow the Single-Infusion Brew Process (see Appendix A).

A Word of Wisdom

To roast barley, spread a measure of pale malt onto a sheet pan. Bake for 15 to 30 minutes in a 350°F oven. Remove from the oven, cool, and store in a paper bag for a couple of weeks to mellow. Boundary Bay Brewery Scotch Ale, Kilt Lifter by the Pike Brewing Company, and Founders Brewing Company Dirty Bastard are all brews akin to Direwolf Ale.

MERMAN'S BLACK STOUT

Lord Manderly (also known at times as Lord Too-Fat-To-Sit-A-Horse) enjoys his food and his drink, especially in vast quantities and served in the company of others. The Lord of White Harbor also ages a fine black stout in his cellars, one that he's only too happy to share in celebration of the great wedding he is to attend in the godswood of Winterfell. Though he may sit with the Starks' enemy to defend his family, the only dark side of Lord Wyman seems to be his taste in stout! (*A Dance with Dragons*, Chapter 37—The Prince of Winterfell)

FOR 5.5 GALLONS AT 1.076, 40 SRM, 34 IBUS, 7.7 PERCENT ABV; 90-MINUTE BOIL

Malt/Grain/Sugar
11.00 pounds Maris Otter Ale Malt
2.00 pounds Flaked Barley
1.00 pound Crystal 60L
0.75 pound Roasted Barley
4.00 ounces Carafa II Special Dehusked Chocolate Malt

Extract (for 10 pounds of Maris Otter Malt)
8.0 pounds Pale Liquid Malt Extract (LME) (Maris Otter Preferable)

Hops
0.88 ounce Target (8.8 percent AA) Pellet for 90 minutes

Other Ingredients
1 tablet Whirlfloc

Yeast
Wyeast 1084 Irish Ale/White Labs WLP004 Irish Ale

MERMAN'S BLACK STOUT

(CONTINUED)

Mash Schedule

Saccharification Rest 155°F 60 minutes

Follow the Single-Infusion Brew Process (see Appendix A).

A WORD OF WISDOM

Adding the hops in for 90 minutes boosts the amount of bitterness extracted from the glands. Going beyond 90-minute boil time, while tempting, produces grassy, vegetal, nasty flavors. Black brews like Boundary Bay Brewery Dry Irish Stout, Founders Brewing Company Kentucky Breakfast Stout, and Rogue Ales Shakespeare Stout could stand head-to-head with Merman's Black Stout on any day.

MANDERLY AUTUMN ALE

If any man in Westeros knows how to pair brews and banquets, it is Lord Manderly of White Harbor. This fine autumn ale is perfect for a harvest feast, letting pumpkin and grains sing farewells to the productive days of summer. As a signature house brew, it's also emblematic of White Harbor's status as a major trading port, combining exotic spices with native ones for an unforgettable warm flavor. (*A Clash of Kings*, Chapter 16—Bran)

FOR 5.5 GALLONS AT 1.054, 14.3 SRM, 23.1 IBUS, 5.3 PERCENT ABV; 60-MINUTE BOIL

Malt/Grain/Sugar
1.81 pounds pumpkin (1 large can)
7.00 pounds Pale Malt Two-Row
2.00 pounds Munich Malt
1.00 pound Crystal 120L
Extract (for 6.00 pounds of Pale Malt)
4.25 pounds Pale Liquid Malt Extract (LME)

Hops
1.00 ounce Tettnanger (4.5 percent AA) Pellet for 60 minutes
0.50 ounce Tettnanger (4.5 percent AA) Pellet for 20 minutes

Other Ingredients
1 tablet Whirlfloc
1 tablespoon Yeast Nutrient
¼ teaspoon cinnamon for 5 minutes
⅛ teaspoon nutmeg for 5 minutes
⅛ teaspoon clove for 5 minutes

Yeast
WLP001 California Ale

MANDERLY AUTUMN ALE

(CONTINUED)

Mash Schedule

Saccharification Rest 152°F 60 minutes

Follow the Single-Infusion Brew Process (see Appendix A).

A Word of Wisdom

Mash the pumpkin with the grain. The exact contribution of pumpkin to the beer's flavor is negligible, but people add it for the romance of it. Used in large enough quantities (and from fresh roasted), you can pick up squash and jalapeño notes. Other autumnal seasonal amber ales include Redhook Ale Brewery Late Harvest Autumn Ale and Magic Hat Brewing Company Roxy Rolles.

LANNISTER GOLD IPA

The true words of the House Lannister are "Hear me roar," but good luck finding someone who doesn't first equate this famly of lions with gold and the practice of paying debts. The Lannisters being the richest family in Westeros, any alcohol made on their land would surely reflect the wealth they are known for. This IPA shines like Lannister armor and has a mineral-driven crispness. If one offered such a drink to Tyrion, he would no doubt insist that only the kitchen staff of Casterly Rock could have created it, on his father's orders. (*A Game of Thrones*, Chapter 5—Jon)

FOR 5.5 GALLONS AT 1.060, 7.3 SRM, 53.8 IBUS, 5.9 PERCENT ABV; 60-MINUTE BOIL

Malt/Grain/Sugar
10.00 pounds Pale Malt Two-Row
1.00 pound Carastan Malt
0.50 pound Munich Malt
Extract (for 9.00 pounds of Pale Malt)
7.00 pounds Pale Liquid Malt Extract (LME)

Hops
0.50 ounce Chinook (13.0 percent AA) Whole for 60 minutes
0.50 ounce Goldings—E.K. (4.75 percent AA) Whole for 60 minutes
0.50 ounce Fuggle (5.0 percent AA) Whole for 60 minutes
0.25 ounce Northern Brewer (9.0 percent AA) Whole for 60 minutes
1.33 ounces Chinook (13.0 percent AA) Whole for 0 minutes

Other Ingredients
1 tablet Whirlfloc
1 tablespoon yeast nutrient
2 tablespoons gypsum salt

Yeast
Wyeast 1056/WLP001 California Ale/US-05 Safale American Ale

LANNISTER GOLD IPA

(CONTINUED)

Mash Schedule

Saccharification Rest 154°F 60 minutes

Follow the Single-Infusion Brew Process (see Appendix A).

A WORD OF WISDOM

Golden IPAs similar to this Lannister brew include New Holland Brewing Company Mad Hatter, Bear Republic Brewing Company Racer 5 IPA, and Asheville Brewing Company Shiva.

BOLTON BASTARD'S PALE ALE

Ramsay Snow may be a bastard, it's true. But that doesn't stop his father Roose Bolton from recognizing him, nor is it going to prevent the man from enjoying a fine pale ale for his own wedding celebration. This one retains the malt focus of a brown ale, unlike many other pale ales, and is as memorable as Ramsay and his own interesting focuses. (*A Dance with Dragons*, Chapter 37—The Prince of Winterfell)

FOR 5.5 GALLONS AT 1.038 OG, 6 SRM, 13 IBUS, 3.2 PERCENT ABV; 60-MINUTE BOIL

Malt/Grain/Sugar
6.00 pounds Maris Otter Ale Malt
1.00 pound Thomas Fawcett Oat Malt
0.50 pound Scottish Crystal 35L
0.50 pound Turbinado ("Raw") Sugar
0.25 pound Belgian Aromatic Malt

Extract (for 5 pounds of Maris Otter Malt)
4.0 pounds Pale Liquid Malt Extract (LME) (Maris Otter Preferable)

Hops
0.25 ounce Wye Target (10.4 percent AA) Pellet for 60 minutes
0.12 ounce Challenger (7.1 percent AA) Pellet for 30 minutes

Other Ingredients
1 tablet Whirlfloc (or 1 teaspoon Irish Moss) added at 20 minutes

Yeast
Wyeast 1275 Thames Valley/Wyeast 1318 London Ale III

Bolton Bastard's Pale Ale

(CONTINUED)

Mash Schedule

Saccharification Rest 152°F 60 minutes

1. Follow the Single-Infusion Brew Process (see Appendix A).
2. Fermentation should take less than a week. Allow the yeast to drop clear (or crash) and package. Carbonate at a lower volume, as mild is not meant to be gassy!

A Word of Wisdom

The once-common oat malt has fallen on hard times. Most famously, it's been used to round out stouts. This recipe uses the oat malt's body-developing creaminess and sweetness to boost flavor and mouthfeel. If you can't find oat malt, substitute flaked oats. For more malt-focused pale ales, try Kona Brewing Company Fire Rock Pale Ale, Independence Brewing Company Independence Pale Ale, and Yazoo Brewing Company Pale Ale.

TARGARYEN DRAGON MEAD

Before she meets Khal Drogo, Daenerys Stormborn is a young girl filled with doubt and fear. A fine mead fit for a dragon helps soothe her in this time of pressure. The dragon mead offered here is a tasty hybrid of a traditional mead and beer. Normally made as a brown barleywine, the basis of this brew is wheat and unforgettably distinct Tupelo honey. Strong, sweet, and fiercely independent from expectations, this brew well characterizes the rebirth of Targaryen leadership. (*A Game of Thrones*, Chapter 3—Daenerys)

FOR 5.5 GALLONS AT 1.120, 3.4 SRM, 27.0 IBUS, 14.0 PERCENT ABV; 60-MINUTE BOIL

Malt/Grain/Sugar
6.0 pounds Wheat Malt
4.0 pounds Pilsner Malt
0.5 pound Cara-Pils Malt
10.00 pounds Tupelo Honey

Extract (for 6 pounds of Wheat Malt and 4 pounds of Pilsner Malt)
8.0 pounds Wheat Liquid Malt Extract (LME)

Hops
2.0 ounces Tettnanger Tettnang (4.3 percent AA) Pellet for 60 minutes

Other Ingredients
1 tablet Whirlfloc
1 tablespoon Yeast Nutrient

Yeast
Red Star Cotes de Blanc White Wine Yeast

Targaryen Dragon Mead

(CONTINUED)

Mash Schedule

Saccharification Rest 150°F 60 minutes

1. Follow the Single-Infusion Brew Process (see Appendix A).
2. Add the honey at the very end of the boil to preserve the aromatics.

A Word of Wisdom

Once kegged and carbonated, there may be a strong odor of diacetyl. This can be scrubbed away by returning the keg to room temperature, venting the CO_2, and adding extra yeast for a few weeks. Or you can try another barleywine like Sierra Nevada Brewing Company Bigfoot Barleywine Style Ale, The Pike Brewing Company Old Bawdy Barley Wine, and Anchor Brewing Company Old Foghorn.

APPENDIX A: Standard Brewing Processes

NOTE: These instructions assume basic knowledge of brewing techniques. For deeper instruction, visit your local homebrew shop.

Single-Infusion Brew Process

Single-infusion mash is the simplest and most versatile mash schedule used extensively in the British and American brewing worlds. This mash regimen takes advantage of the complete conversion of modern barley malt. Before developing better strains of barley and malting techniques, more complicated mash regimens were needed to convert the mash.

SINGLE-STEP-INFUSION MASH

1. Measure out water based on the amount of malt you're using. Typically you'll use 1.25 quarts per pound of malt. (So, for 10 pounds of malt you'll use 12.5 quarts of water.) This is your strike water. In a separate vessel, measure an equal or greater volume of water. This is called your sparge water.

2. Heat the strike water to approximately 12°F above the desired mash rest temperature specified in the recipe. (For instance, heat to 164°F for a mash rest of 152°F.) Also heat the sparge water to 170°F.

3. Mix your grains thoroughly into the strike water, and stir to break up any clumps. Rest for 10 minutes and take a temperature. Adjust with cold or hot water (or direct heat in a pot) to settle to the rest temperature. This is your mash.

4. After 60 minutes, slowly drain out a quart of cloudy grainy liquid from the strike water (this runoff is called wort). Gently pour the wort back into the mash. Continue this process until the wort runs clear.

5. Divert the clear wort to a boil kettle, and continue to top off the mash with hot sparge water until the water stays approximately 1 inch above the grain bed. This process is called sparging.

6. Collect 5 gallons of wort in the boil kettle, then stop adding sparge water. Continue to collect wort until the boil kettle contains the target volume plus 1 gallon for every 60 minutes of boiling (for example, you'll need 6.5 gallons in the boil kettle for a 5.5-gallon recipe boiled for one hour). Let mash cool. Bring beer in boil kettle to a boil.

7. Once beer boils, begin timing your boil and add hops as specified in the recipe. For instance, add the 60-minutes hops when 60 minutes are remaining in the boil. (This is typically the start of the boil, but some recipes do specify longer boils of 75 to 120 minutes. Once the water boils, start counting down and when you hit 60, add the hops.)

8. At boil's end, add any last-minute hop additions. Vigorously stir the pot to create a whirlpool effect, place the lid on, and wait 10 minutes. Chill the beer to 60°F to 75°F with a chiller.

9. Transfer the beer to the fermenter. Take a gravity sample with a hydrometer and record. Add aeration or oxygenation and then pitch yeast.

10. Refer to the Fermentation and Packaging section of this appendix to finish brew.

Multistep Brew Process

Older malts and the few undermodified malts left on the market require more complicated mash rests. Belgian breweries often employ a multistep mash to encourage more attenuative worts. Make sure you are comfortable with the Single-Step-Infusion Mash process before trying a multistep brew, as they are more complicated and advanced.

MULTISTEP MASH INSTRUCTIONS

1. Begin as in the Single-Infusion process. Complete your first rest at the lower temperature (up to Step 3).
2. Begin to raise the mash temperature by infusion. Refer to Calculations in this appendix to determine the amount of water needed to raise the temperature of the mash from the first rest temperature to the next one.
3. Repeat Step 2 for as many rests as required. When the last rest is completed, resume the Single-Infusion Process at Step 4.

Fermentation and Packaging

1. For most normal-gravity beers, allow the beer to ferment in primary for a week or two until the gravity is no longer changing. Fermentation temperature should be varied to the optimum values indicated by the yeast manufacturer.
2. To bottle, clean and sanitize fifty-four 12-ounce bottles.
3. Prepare a sugar solution of ¾ cup (approx 4.5 ounces by weight) priming (corn) sugar and ¾ cup filtered water. Boil for 10 to 15 minutes and add to sanitized bottling bucket.
4. Siphon beer into bottling bucket (also known as racking) to mix sugar solution thoroughly.
5. Fill each bottle to approximately 1.5 to 2 fingers' width from the top and cap.
6. Store bottles in the seventies for two weeks. Chill one bottle and check the carbonation level. Wait one more week if carbonation is not as desired.

Calculations

Strike Water Temperature

$$\text{Strike Water Temperature} = (\text{Mash}_{\text{Factor}} - \text{Grain}_{\text{Factor}}) / \text{Volume}_{\text{Gallons Water}}$$

Example: Find the temperature needed for a mash with 10 pounds of grain, 12 quarts of strike water, and a desired rest temperature of 153°F

$\text{Weight}_{\text{Grain}}$ = 10 pounds

$\text{Temperature}_{\text{Grain}}$ = 70°F

$\text{Volume}_{\text{Gallons Strike Water}}$ = 3.0 gallons

$\text{Temperature}_{\text{Mash}}$ = 153°F

$\text{Mash}_{\text{Specific Heat}}$ = (10 × 0.05) + 3

$\text{Mash}_{\text{Factor}}$ = 3.5 × 153 = 535.5

$\text{Grain}_{\text{Specific Heat}}$ = 10 × 0.05 = 0.5

$\text{Grain}_{\text{Factor}}$ = 0.5 × 70 = 35

Strike Water Temperature = (535.5 – 35) / 3 = 166.8°F

Mash Infusion Equation

How much boiling water is needed raise a mash to the next temperature? The equation depends on the differences in temperature between known temps.

$\text{Temperature}_{\text{Mash-Grain}} = \text{Temperature}_{\text{Mash}} - \text{Temperature}_{\text{Grain}}$

$\text{Temperature}_{\text{Mash-Strike}} = \text{Temperature}_{\text{Mash}} - \text{Temperature}_{\text{Strike Water}}$

$\text{Temperature}_{\text{Boil-Mash}} = \text{Temperature}_{\text{BoilingWater}} - \text{Temperature}_{\text{Mash}}$

$\text{Total Heat}_{\text{Grain}} = \text{Grain}_{\text{Specific Heat}} \times \text{Temperature}_{\text{Mash-Grain}}$

$\text{Total Heat}_{\text{Strike Water}} = \text{Volume}_{\text{Gallons Strike Water}} \times \text{Temperature}_{\text{Mash-Strike}}$

$\text{Volume}_{\text{Boiling Water}} = (\text{Total Heat}_{\text{Grain}} + \text{Total Heat}_{\text{Strike Water}}) / \text{Temperature}_{\text{Boil-Mash}}$

Example: Boost the previous mash to 168°F with boiling water (210°F for heat loss).

$\text{Temperature}_{\text{Mash}}$ = 168°F

$\text{Temperature}_{\text{Mash-Grain}}$ = 168°F – 70°F = 98°F

$\text{Temperature}_{\text{Mash-Strike}}$ = 168°F – 166.8°F = 1.2°F

$\text{Temperature}_{\text{Boil-Mash}}$ = 210°F – 168°F = 42°F

$\text{Total Heat}_{\text{Grain}}$ = 0.5 × 98°F = 49°F

$\text{Total Heat}_{\text{Strike Water}}$ = 3.0 gallons × 1.2°F = 3.6

$\text{Volume}_{\text{Boiling Water}}$ = (49 + 3.6) / 42 = 1.25 gallons

Appendix B: Recipes by Region

In a world connected by ancient roads, ocean passages, and sharp tradesmen, food travels widely—for a price. A meal enjoyed at a pub is likely a good example of local fare, but a king's banquet may also boast the bounty of his allies abroad and costly delights from exotic realms.

Knowing where recipes likely originated can help identify flavors that might play well off of each other, even though characters in A Song of Ice and Fire may have enjoyed them nearly a world away. Ser Barristan may have feasted on Wild Boar Ribs with Dragon Pepper (Chapter 5) in King's Landing, but it's the heat of Dornish dragon peppers that make the dish unique. Some recipes are too commonly eaten to truly pinpoint and have been given a more general area of origin—like Westrosian Barley Bread (Chapter 3). Other recipes owe their flavors to more than one region, including Ten Towers Cold Beef and Oldtown Mustard (Chapter 2) with origins in the Iron Islands and the Reach. Finally, there will always be foods mentioned very generally in A Song of Ice and Fire that have more specific ties to locations here; in those cases, the recipes are always listed in the regions that inspired the particular twist this book gives them.

Combine your experience with the characters, references to chapters from A Song of Ice and Fire, and this appendix to craft menus inspired by your favorite characters and settings in Westeros and beyond.

WESTEROS

Dreadfort
Bolton Bastard's Pale Ale (Chapter 6)

The Riverlands
Tywin Lannister's Garlic Sausage (Chapter 1)
Road to Riverrun Apple Chips (Chapter 2)
Inn at the Crossroads 7-Grain Loaf (Chapter 3)
Trident Flax and Fennel Hardbread (Chapter 3)
Inn of the Kneeling Man's Rabbit Stew
    (Chapter 4)

Harrenhal
Weasel's Oatcakes (Chapter 1)
Harrenhal Vegetable Stew (Chapter 4)

Riverrun
Jeyne's Stewed Onions and Leeks (Chapter 3)
Riverrun Turnip Greens and Red Fennel Salad
    (Chapter 4)
Brynden Tully's Blackened Trout with Dornish
    Gremolata (Chapter 5)

The Twins
Late Lord Frey's Leek Soup (Chapter 4)
Lord Walder's Green Bean Salad (Chapter 4)

The Vale
The Eyrie
Mord's Boiled Beans (Chapter 3)
The Vale Summer Berries and Cream Tart
    (Chapter 6)

Gates of the Moon
Lord Nestor Royce's Wild Mushroom Ragout
    (Chapter 4)
Sweetrobin's Stewed Goat (Chapter 4)

The Three Sisters
Sister's Stew (Chapter 4)

The Fingers
Littlefinger's Lamprey Pie (Chapter 5)

The Iron Islands
Harlaw
Ten Towers Cold Beef and Oldtown Mustard
    (Chapter 2)

Pyke
Pyke Onion Pie (Chapter 5)

The Westerlands
Casterly Rock
Golden Lions' Spiced Squash (Chapter 3)
Tyrion's Leg of Lamb (Chapter 5)
Lannister Beef with Horseradish (Chapter 5)
Lannister Gold IPA (Chapter 6)

The Reach
The Hedge Knight's Salt Beef Salami (Chapter 2)

Oldtown
Grand Maester Pycelle's Prized Pomegranate
    Grapefruit Bars (Chapter 2)
Ten Towers Cold Beef and Oldtown Mustard
    (Chapter 2)

The Arbor
Redwyne Brown Stock (Chapter 4)

Bitterbridge
Lord Caswell's Venison and Barley Stew
    (Chapter 4)
Bitterbridge Blackberry Tart (Chapter 6)

Horn Hill
Samwell's Blueberry Ricotta Tart (Chapter 6)

ACROSS THE NARROW SEA

Soft Flatbread from Across the Narrow Sea
    (Chapter 3)

Free Cities

BRAAVOS

The Blind Girl's Piping Hot Fish and Pepper
    Breakfast (Chapter 1)
Braavosian Frog Legs (Chapter 3)
Umma's Morning Loaf (Chapter 3)
House of Black and White's Golden Coin
    (Chapter 6)

PENTOS

Illyrio's Goose Liver Drowned in Wine
    (Chapter 2)
The Cheesemonger's Candied Onions
    (Chapter 2)
Pentoshi Stinky Cheese Plate (Chapter 2)
Pentoshi Mushrooms in Butter and Garlic
    (Chapter 3)
Illyrio's Buttered Parsnip Purée (Chapter 3)
Dothraki Duck (Chapter 5)
Pentoshi Crisp Fingerfish (Chapter 5)

VOLANTIS

Volantene Honey Sausages (Chapter 2)
Volantene Cold Beet Soup (Chapter 4)
Bittersweet Volantene Stout (Chapter 6)

LYS

Saan's Minced Lamb with Pepper (Chapter 5)
Tears of Lys (Chapter 6)
The Strangler (Chapter 6)

Dothraki Sea

Khaleesi's Heart (Chapter 5)

Slaver's Bay

Balerion Fish Roe Dip (Chapter 2)

Ghiscar

Ghiscari Spiced Honeyed Locusts (Chapter 2)

Meereen

Queen of Meereen's Persimmon Crumble Ice
    Cream (Chapter 6)

Index

About the Author

ALAN KISTLER is a Peruvian-Irish American who was born in Washington D.C., has lived in New York City for over a decade, and has been known by the nickname of "Sizzler" for even longer. Alan is an actor who usually makes a living writing from his laptop (oftentimes while he's sitting in a bar). His weekly column "Agent of S.T.Y.L.E." is featured on Newsarama.com and focuses on the evolution of superheroes and villains. He is the creator and a co-host of the weekly podcast *Crazy Sexy Geeks*, which discusses popular geek culture, deals out dating advice, and has filmed several online videos under the same label.

Alan has been recognized as a comic book historian by major media and news outlets. Through his articles and convention appearances, he has earned a reputation for a deep knowledge of many science fiction and fantasy sagas, as well as different mythologies. He has appeared in comic book documentaries for Warner Bros. Home Video and has spoken at the Paley Center on multiple occasions concerning Star Trek, the history of science fiction television, time travel stories, and vampire fiction. He has also spoken and written often concerning the need for a stronger portrayal of women in films and television. Alan has inspired the creation of a fictional counterpart in Star Trek novels by David A. Mack, "Protection Agent Alan Kistler."

He regularly links his newest projects and articles to his site, AlanKistler.com, and enjoys communicating with fans through his Twitter account: @SizzlerKistler. He knows far too much about superheroes, Doctor Who, vampires, the Rat Pack, and British comedies. Alan believes Isaac Asimov should be required reading in schools.

Contains material adapted and abridged from: